DATE DUE

*Managing
the New Generation
in Business*

Managing the New Generation in Business

THOMAS F. STROH

College of Business and Public Administration
Florida Atlantic University, Boca Raton, Florida

McGRAW-HILL BOOK COMPANY

New York   St. Louis   San Francisco   Düsseldorf   Johannesburg
Kuala Lumpur   London   Mexico   Montreal   New Delhi
Panama   Rio de Janeiro   Singapore   Sydney   Toronto

SPONSORING EDITOR   Dale L. Dutton
DIRECTOR OF PRODUCTION   Stephen J. Boldish
EDITING SUPERVISORS   Barbara Church/Carolyn Nagy
DESIGNER   Naomi Auerbach
EDITING AND PRODUCTION STAFF   Gretlyn Blau,
    Teresa F. Leaden, George E. Oechsner

MANAGING THE NEW GENERATION IN BUSINESS

07-062195-0

1234567890 VBVB 754321

Preface

WHEN MEMBERS of the new generation enter the establishments of business, industry, associations, government, and education, they pose a real threat of change to the establishments. Paradoxically, they also offer hope for the betterment of both the establishments and the managers and executives who now run them. This brief study was written primarily for men in management in American organizations, from first-line supervisors to top executives. Executives concerned with manpower planning, personnel, and training and development should be particularly interested in the specific suggestions contained in this book.

The author does not defend the actions of members of the angry and frustrated new generation but attempts to explain them because understanding precedes managing these

v

knowledgeable and energetic young people. Nor does he defend the establishment which may use archaic traditional management principles and therefore, be doomed to stifle its own growth. The author attacks both the new generation and the establishment, attempting to point out when, where, and how things can be improved by the two antagonists.

Because many diverse concepts of management have been published, this work is also intended to serve as a guide to all instructors and students of management in institutions from two-year community colleges through graduate schools. Major management theories often seem contradictory and merely stylish, although the advocates of each extreme theory can cite some successful experiences in using their own brand of principles. Clearly, different situations require different principles of management; thus each concept, properly applied, can contribute to a better understanding of modern management principles.

This work is intentionally brief, optimistic, and hard-hitting for the benefit of the busy executive in the real world. It is also a distillation of many fine and detailed management studies which any serious student can pursue at his own pace as directed in this work. Managers and academicians should be able to take exception to some of the author's interpretations and conclusions on the basis of their broad knowledge rather than isolated individual experience. It is the author's intention to cause the reader to think along positive lines of living together rather than along negative lines of damning the opposite position.

The author is deeply indebted to Jared F. Harrison,

Corporate Training Director of the International Paper Company, Joel Aron, Executive Vice-president of Personnel Testing Service, Inc., and Robert Vizza, Dean of the School of Business of Manhattan College, for their special insights into both the new generation and the establishment. Special thanks is also acknowledged to a young teaching colleague, Thomas Zimmerer, for research assistance and to three other "young tigers," Bob and Heide Welke and Richard Signore, who seriously debated points in the manuscript and, with good humor, contributed the original artwork. Of course, the author accepts sole responsibility for errors of omission and commission in the final work.

Thomas F. Stroh

Contents

*Managing
the New Generation
in Business*

CHAPTER ONE

Who Needs Them?

MUCH IS WRITTEN TODAY about the widening gap between generations. One business executive has been quoted directly in the press about the young hippie who looks, smokes, and acts like the late Che Guevara. This executive asks, "Is he in support of our economic system or is he in *sub rosa* revolt?" [1] Clearly, he would not hire such a person.

Many executives allude to their basic distrust of anyone who tries to look like Fidel Castro, and they insist that the new generation conform to their own clean-shaven executive image. Their position is one of a stern parent who demands the child obey or be punished. Their organization could not hire a misfit or tolerate an employee who did not fit the organizational image.

[1] Gerry G. Germain, "Bar Door To Hippies," *Advertising Age*, June 23, 1969, p. 2.

More moderate executives excuse the excessive behavior of youth today by remembering their own overexuberant college capers, from flagpole sitting and swallowing goldfish to dormitory raids for the girls' panties. Each generation has its periods of defiance and wants to remake the world. The more moderate executives see today's youth as being noisy but completely normal and expect the "widening gap" to close automatically when youth enters business.

Student protests are nothing new. Of the six presidents who served Yale University during its founding years, three had resigned by 1776 due to student opposition.

A prominent sociologist, Dr. Robert Nisbet, recently wrote, "The student revolution is collapsing because most American college students are children of the middle class and are not dedicated and disciplined to meet the demanding life of the hard-core revolutionary." [2] But he contends that the leaders of campus agitation, although clever enough to hoodwink many adults, have not been able to bring off a genuine revolution because they don't really have a cause noble enough to call forth lasting devotion and sacrifice.

Essentially, executives feel the extreme hippies represent only a small part of today's youth, perhaps less than 2 percent of those under twenty-five years of age. They feel that if this small element does not change to conform to business standards it should be ostracized. They contend that the country and the economy cannot be destroyed by an

[2] As quoted by Louis Cassels, United Press International senior editor, in the *Fort Lauderdale News*, Feb. 27, 1970, from an article written by Dr. Robert Nisbet for a British magazine, *Encounter*.

outraged minority. These executive groups strongly feel that the 98 percent of today's youth that seeks an education should not be blocked by the 2 percent minority that wishes to tear down the establishment.

THE CREDIBILITY GAP

While such reasoning may seem logical on the surface, it serves to illustrate the truly widening and dangerous credibility gap between generations. The futility of such generalizations is indicated when one searches into the feelings of the *majority* of youth today and discovers that at least 70 percent not only tolerate but are willing to defend and support the 1 or 2 percent who are extremists! The members of this majority will not change when they enter a company with typical and traditional management.

Then why should an executive who has the power and responsibility to hire and promote young people consider employing such potentially disruptive people? In other words, who needs them?

POPULATION STATISTICS

Objective, cold statistics give the answer. Prior to 1900 the nation's population approximately doubled every twenty-five years. The population expansion slowed substantially during the depressed decade of the 1930s, when the birthrate declined. After World War II there was a "baby

Who needs them?

boom" lasting through the 1950s. As shown in Figure 1-1, in the 1950s the number of Americans rose by 28 million, or by 18.6 percent. In the 1960s, the number of Americans rose by about 26 million. The projected gain of 27 million in the next decade, or by 1980, figures out to 13.2 percent.

By 1980, more than half the population will again be

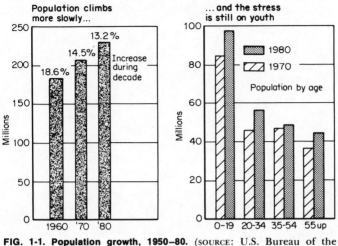

FIG. 1-1. Population growth, 1950–80. (SOURCE: U.S. Bureau of the Census.)

under thirty, with an increase in college enrollments. Twenty years ago only 1 young adult in 18 was a college graduate. Today 1 in 6 has a college degree. By 1975, the number of bachelor's degrees will have increased by 73 percent while the number of master's degrees will have jumped by 90 percent.

Management must now consider the age composition of the population. The middle-age group, aged thirty-five to fifty-four, will *not* grow in line with the rest of the population. This is the group that provides the managers for business and industry. By the year 1980, there will be only a small gain in the group aged thirty-five to forty-four and an actual drop in the group from forty-five to fifty-four.

TABLE 1-1   *Ages 18–24 of Total Population*

Year	Population	%, total population
1869–70	4,574,000	1.14
1879	7,092,000	1.63
1889	8,820,000	1.78
1899	10,357,000	2.29
1909–10	12,300,000	2.89
1919–20	12,830,000	4.66
1929–30	15,280,000	7.20
1939–40	16,458,000	9.08
1949–50	16,120,000	16.50
1959–60	15,693,000	20.49
Fall, 1963	18,152,000	23.33

SOURCE: U.S. Bureau of the Census.

BUSINESS GROWTH

While this favored group is diminishing, business expansion goes on unabatedly, and plans in many industries call for double or triple growth in the next decade. Corporate goals of a 20 percent annual growth are both common and attainable. But for a number of years manpower shortages have been getting more drastic. For example, the shortage of computer programmers has driven their wage scale out of proportion to their qualifications. The long period of a shortage of salesmen has now generated a critical shortage of sales *managers!* This picture is repeated in a majority of occupations in which planned shortages of qualified professionals have been used as an economic tool. Roy W. Walters estimates that United States corporations need 200,000 potential managers *right now*.[3]

[3] Roy W. Walters, "Where Can We Get More Managers?" *Training in Business and Industry,* August, 1969, p. 25.

If one projects the population composition trends, statistics show by 1975 there will be a shortage of people in the age bracket from thirty-five to forty-four, from which higher executives are normally chosen. The National Industrial Conference Board's report "The Consumer of the Seventies" foretells a decade of impressive growth and change. The population of young adults will grow twice as fast as the total population. Personal income will increase by more than 50 percent, and per capita spending power by two-fifths.

The twentieth century has been described as "the most amazingly progressive 100 years, from the technical standpoint, in the history of man." [4] People who will be here in the year 2000 are *already* in our schools, and by the turn of the century they will be only thirty-five to fifty years old—the prime age for management!

This authority further states:

> The breakthroughs that have been witnessed just in the past five years have led to greater demands for trained personnel in research, development, and for the production and services in all fields of applied science. At present, estimates show that there should be five technicians for each engineer or physical scientist; six to ten technicians for each medical doctor or researcher in the health fields; and four to five technicians for each biological scientist. We do not come near these needed ratios. [5]

In 1900, for example, there was 1 health assistant for every doctor. In 1970 the ratio is approximately 1 for every

[4] Charles S. Jensen, "Wanted: Manpower for Utopia," *S.A.M. Advanced Management Journal*, vol. 34, no. 3, p. 14, July, 1969.
[5] *Ibid.*

13 doctors. By 1975, it is expected there will be 1 for every 25 doctors. The problem of expanding knowledge and technology has caused similar deteriorating ratios in many other fields of endeavor.

Combine this lag in the number of people in the desired age brackets with the intended expansion of business. Then superimpose the growing demand for managers in education and governmental areas, and one begins to see the answer to the question "Who needs these young people?" We all do!

Yes sir, what can you do for us?

WHAT ARE YOUNG
PEOPLE LIKE?

What are these people from eighteen to twenty-four years old like? They were born after World War II; hence most have been raised on better diets than previous generations. The knowledge of the value of vitamins together with an affluent society has permitted them to eat better and grow stronger and larger than any other generation in our history. Medical knowledge and inoculations against diseases have permitted them to become the healthiest generation to date. Research has created more knowledge and methodologies to permit mass education at a higher level than had been possible in any earlier generation. As a group, these young people are more knowledgeable than their parents were at the same age.

In an American Council on Education survey of 245,156 entering freshmen at 358 colleges and universities, 52.4 percent of the freshmen said that in the past year they had drunk beer and 59.1 percent said that they had taken vitamins.[6]

Every year about 1 family in 5 in the United States moves its home. Such high mobility has exposed our youth to many cultures and different social situations. Young people are socially intelligent well beyond the level of prior generations at the same age. Sex education, the pill, and a permissive society have combined to produce a generation

[6] *Degree Data,* Jan. 1, 1969.

TABLE 1-2   *Level of School Completed by Persons 25 Years Old and Over*

Year	Less than 5 yr, elementary school, %	4 yr or more, high school, %	4 yr or more, college, %	Median completed school yr, %
1910	23.8	13.5	2.7	8.1
1920	22.0	16.4	3.3	8.2
1930	17.5	19.1	3.9	8.4
1940	13.5	24.1	4.6	8.6
1950	10.8	33.4	6.0	9.3
1960	8.3	41.1	7.7	10.5
1967	6.1	51.1	10.1	12.0

SOURCE: U.S. Department of Health, Education, and Welfare, *Digest of Educational Statistics 1968,* Government Printing Office, Washington, 1968, p. 9.

which can enjoy pleasures but is also able to turn its attention to more serious matters without crippling pangs of hunger, regret, or guilt.

As a group, today's kids are bigger, healthier, more knowledgeable, and often more moral than any prior generation. They have been *told* that spinach tastes good, medical shots do not hurt, and hard work builds good character. Yet, their personal experience has often shown that there are true differences between what authorities say occurs and reality. Authorities dispense information which is not always factual. The trick is to discover when the dispenser of information is telling the truth and when he is misleading youth for the authority's selfish benefit. These young sophisticates have heard Mom complain about housework but have seen her drinking cocktails and playing bridge all afternoon. They have heard Dad complain about slaving at the office to support his family, but they have seen the matchbook covers he brings home from the go-go places and the topless-waitress restaurants. These youngsters are intelligent and sophisticated enough to question any authority, because adults have taught them to do so! For example, the author's school, Florida Atlantic University, does not want to produce academics who accept the status quo uncritically but to produce citizens who are not afraid to question present conditions and to question accepted conclusions.

Indeed, a number of executives have been known to maintain Greenwich Village "pads" where they can mix with the young hippies. Because young people read the advertisements for false beards and sideburns, they recognize the weekend swinger as the hypocrite who shows up Monday morning clean-shaven in the executive suite.

As noted earlier, of all people in the United States twenty-five years old and over in 1967, 51.1 percent had completed four years of high school or more. In our affluent society, with low-tuition colleges for the masses, 75 percent of those in grade school will graduate from high school and 40 percent will go to college. Note in Figure 1-2 how education for the masses is accelerating.

MANAGEMENT PROBLEMS WITH
EXISTING SUBORDINATES

With the current shortage of good management people, which is projected to become more acute, there are many problems with existing subordinates. Typical people prob-

For every ten pupils in 5th grade in 1959 to 1960

9.7 entered the 9th grade in 1963 to 1964

8.5 entered the 11th grade in 1965 to 1966

7.2 graduated from high school in 1967

4.0 entered college in fall 1967

2.0 are likely to earn 4-year degree in 1971

FIG. 1-2. Estimated retention rates, fifth grade through college graduation, 1959–71. (SOURCE: U.S. Department of Health, Education, and Welfare, *Digest of Educational Statistics 1968,* Washington, 1968, p. 9.)

lems raised in management seminars conducted by the author in 1970 included the following:

E. W.: "I have a man with a record of ten years' satisfactory experience who has let down on his job. He seems more interested in outside activities, and now his job performance is poor.

H. H.: "I have a comptroller, with us for twenty years, who won't accept our new costing standards. He feels we have singled out his plant to make trouble."

G. F.: "For five years I trained a subordinate to replace me. He was offered a promotion, but before it took place, things changed and the offer had to be withdrawn. Now he wants to quit!"

R. M.: "I was put in charge of a group of senior men who resent my inexperience. They seem to accept my technical competence, but they are sullen and uncooperative."

J. M.: "As a plant foreman, I am glad when I can get 90 to 100 percent performance out of my machine operators. I have one man who consistently performed at 140 percent for two years, then suddenly dropped to 90 percent. How can I get him back up to where he had been? The union pay scale is the same."

D. J.: "One of my supervisors was made foreman of a thirty-man shop. He now works twelve hours a day and still cannot handle the scheduling and communications required. Should I fire him?"

W. B.: "My subordinate has done a great job assuming responsibility and really turning out good work. The other day, for no apparent reason, he blew his top and said he wished I would fire him. What should a manager do in such a situation?"

B. R.: "My administration estimator had been doing an excellent job for many months. Now he seems to be avoiding responsibility, and he is becoming hard to get along with in the sales department."

D. M.: "I put a young, well-educated man in charge of our sales service operation, and he handled it very well for a short period; but he seems to lose interest quickly, and if I didn't pep him up, his job performance would deteriorate."

W. W.: "I have an effective salesman with three years' experience who has grown complacent and is now unhappy with his job and suspicious of all levels of management. What can I do with him?"

D. W.: "I've promoted a good man, but he can't seem to get along with people. Either he does the subordinate's job himself or he does nothing. He is absent a lot, and his drinking is becoming a problem."

J. S.: "Two of my subordinates had been well trained for higher jobs. When one got promoted, the other, an equally good man, started talking about leaving."

W. N.: "Our union steward tries to run our shop. Since he has had family problems at home, he now blows up every minor problem into a major one. I can't fire him, so how do I cope with such a problem?"

W. R.: "My subordinates were very cooperative until I got a new boss. Now my men go over my head directly to my boss, and I have to spend most of my time getting the facts after the boss has heard only half-truths."

These successful managers in business and industry reported many variations of the same people problems. The managers ranged from first-line supervisors all the way up to corporate officers. Their experience and knowledge levels also ranged over the complete spectrum. These men were fearful and suspicious about the new generation's campus activities and attitudes toward business in general. Those who were optimistic felt the new generation would be no worse than their existing subordinates, while some who were pessimistic felt overwhelmed by the problems they anticipated in supervising the new generation.

EXECUTIVE COLLEGES

Dean C. Miller, writing for United Press International, datelined New York, March 3, 1970, reports on in-house college-level programs to hone existing executives for bigger jobs and promising youngsters for managerial positions. His article describes the Motorola Executive Institute in Vail, Arizona, and mentions similar schools of International Business Machines at Sands Point, New York, and General Electric at Ossining, New York. Many large corporations have an education budget larger than that of a typical university, testifying to their recognition of the problem and their faith in education.

Dr. William Bakrow, Motorola Executive Institute president, is quoted, "Our objective is balanced personal growth and avoidance of the drop in formative learning ability that often occurs as a man moves into his early forties." [7] The curriculum includes management sciences, information technology, international economics, group dynamics, origins of philosophical movements, and development of polit-

[7] Dean C. Miller, "Executive College Grads Climb Ladder," *Fort Lauderdale News,* Mar. 3, 1970, p. 16A.

ical thought. Clearly, their graduates should be more aware of world and group situations.

Such massive and expensive programs point up the current shortage of managers and the need to deal with the real problem of executives' becoming obsolete before they are expected to retire. Executives are being made aware of their social and moral responsibilities to the world. Such responsibilities may not have been stressed a generation ago, but they are closely related to much of the noise we hear from students on college campuses today.

CONCLUSIONS

As a group, the new generation is bigger, healthier, and more knowledgeable than prior generations. Young people smoke less and drink no more than their parents did at the same age. They have read about prior generations making war to end all wars, war to make the world safe for democracy, and war to free people who did not want to be free; economic trusts that exploit people; freedom given only lip service as far as several minority groups are concerned; and the disclosure of bribes and graft in the highest and most respected offices in government. If they are impatient and suspicious, surely it should not be a surprise.

Today's young people have learned to accept atomic power, jet aircraft, a round trip to the moon, and instant communication around the world. They have not accepted poverty, starvation, race superiority, polluted air and water, and war—particularly if there is any possibility of someone in authority realizing a selfish gain from these conditions.

The new generation, in many ways, is superior to and suspicious of prior generations. Its members are not bad or immoral kids, but they are different. Somehow, we, the older people, must communicate with them because we need them and, it will be shown, they also need us.

CHAPTER TWO

Today's Attitudes and Existing Motivation

WHAT IS A TYPICAL COLLEGE SENIOR'S ATTITUDE toward a business career? Annual surveys beginning before the Vietnam war and continuing to 1970 tend to repeat the same general lack of interest in business, if not an outright distaste for joining business.[1] Typically, less than one-third of the seniors are seriously *considering* a career in business, and less than 15 percent state business is their first choice. The students' main concern about entering a business corporation is a fear that companies allow too little freedom to effect changes for the betterment of society and that the profit motivation drives business to do things that cause or contribute to social ills.

[1] Lou Harris, *Newsweek*, May 2, 1966; *Wall Street Journal*, Oct. 12, 1967; *Time*, July 18, 1969; *Associated Press*, Princeton, N.J., Mar. 21, 1970.

19

More college seniors want to make a career in education than to make a career in business. More seniors prefer the Peace Corps than prefer business. Only half the college seniors feel business is financially rewarding and competitive. Not more than 1 in 5 college seniors feels that business will be a challenge for his energy, knowledge, and intelligence. Only 1 in 10 seniors feels business will offer him a chance to be creative, and fewer than 1 in 10 feels that business will be intellectually stimulating.

Perhaps the key statistic which highlights both youth's attitude and present motivation is that only *1* college senior *in 100* feels that business offers him a chance to help others.

Yet these young men and women are realistic in that they know most of them will someday end up in business. They prefer to do their thing—help ghetto children or campaign for peace or change some establishment, something noble and unselfish—and then are resigned to drift into business. They expect to be bored in a business career but are confident they will make a good living.

Students who are business majors and, to a lesser extent, students in graduate schools of business reflect most of these same attitudes. This would seem to indicate the problem is not simply one of education but more a problem of communication.

NEGATIVE MOTIVATORS

The polls clearly indicate today's youth does *not* seek money as a *primary* goal. Raised in an affluent society where unions have earned a guaranteed good wage for unskilled labor, they feel quite confident they can earn a comfortable living whenever they choose. Inflation is an economic condition which they consider the normal way of life because they have studied labor contracts with cost-of-living escalator clauses. Since World War II the rate of inflation in the United States has been 2 percent annually, and it is forecast to accelerate in the next decade.

Discipline is another traditional form of motivation and one that seems to come easiest to many supervisors and managers: "You will do as I say because I am the boss." A generation ago or more, children were taught at home and at school to show strict obedience to their elders. Later, as young adults they found little difficulty in adjusting to stern discipline in the office or factory. During the depression of the thirties, many people willingly worked under strict authoritarian discipline because of fear of losing their jobs.

Recent years have seen an increased standard of living and nearly full employment. Our children have been brought up in a permissive society. Freedom and self-expression are encouraged in the home. Churches and schools emphasize spontaneous discussion and individual expression. Dogma is examined for its meaning to the individual, and in the process basic values are questioned. As a consequence, the young graduate finds it hard to accept autocratic leadership and discipline on the job.

Instead of reacting positively to discipline, the young graduate will feel such leadership tactics simply prove his suspicion that work is menial and without purpose. Given this climate, he will try to get away with doing as little as he can. Discipline requires close supervision, or telling every worker exactly what he must do every minute with pressure constantly applied to do a better job. Research studies have shown most groups of workers react negatively to constant close supervision.

MANAGEMENT BY OBJECTIVES

A more sophisticated version of traditional discipline is "management by objectives." In theory, the subordinate and his manager together agree on goals which can be attained. Criteria for performance for an individual or group should be decided jointly in advance. According to George S. Odiorne, this process has two advantages.[2] First, it permits the followers to participate in determining on what basis their efforts will be judged. Second, involving the followers in the planning process will increase their commitment to the goals and objectives which are established. Odiorne's cycle of management by objectives is reprinted in Figure 2-1 to symbolize this theory.

Unfortunately, in applying this theory it is common practice for top management to decide on a set of goals or objectives for each subordinate unit and then to exert constant pressure and harassment to ensure that these goals are met. Superiors telephone, demanding to know why objectives are not being met. Putting a man on the carpet is also

[2] George S. Odiorne, *Management by Objectives*, Pitman, New York, 1964.

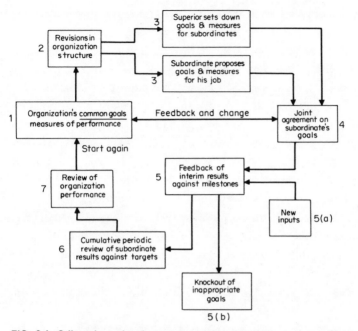

FIG. 2-1. Odiorne's cycle of management by objectives. (SOURCE: George S. Odiorne, *Management by Objectives,* Pitman, New York, 1964.)

a common means of abusing his efforts. The penalty for not achieving goals is usually the withholding of promotions or salary increases, if not outright dismissal.

One large paper company has a "goals program" which operates as a top management club to force subordinates to think as they are told. Subordinates submit their goals and objectives for a coming year without any guidelines from above. Their first effort is rejected with very minor indications of what top management wants. Second, third, and additional versions are submitted and rejected in turn. One division of this company, with sales in excess of $100 million, recently operated without approved goals for six months. More than half of the game had passed before the subordinates were told where the goalpost was located!

Another company, with sales in excess of $1 billion annually, uses "deviation from standard" as its whip. Whenever a manager's performance falls below a prearranged norm, he must explain why it is off and what steps he is taking to prevent a reoccurrence of the deviation. When production machines break down, the managers get ulcers. When sales are off in an entire industry, the sales managers of this one company are forced to double their efforts and working hours to approach the present goals. This kind of pressure or discipline causes many of the familiar psychosomatic illnesses. It also causes high blood pressure, strokes, and heart attacks.

Conversely, when a plant machine works faster than anticipated, the production manager can "bank" some of the excess in case of future breakdowns. When an entire industry realizes a seller's market, the sales manager can play golf two or three days a week. Men in middle management learn to live with the goals system, but they do not enjoy their jobs, and they do not realize any personal satisfaction of achieving. They do not grow and develop mentally and often will *avoid* a challenging job in the future.

When the young graduate is put under too much pressure of this kind, he becomes frustrated and may find it difficult to make intelligent decisions. He may revert to horseplay or simply give up trying altogether. Alcohol and dope become escapes from the rat race. In any case, production suffers, and a potentially good young person is wasted. Today's young graduates respond negatively to traditional discipline.

With almost full employment, our young people know they can easily switch jobs if they feel frustrated or stymied in an organization. Being highly mobile they can readily switch industries and move freely throughout the country. Loyalty is not apt to be placed the first few years in a job, particularly when young men enter business with sincere doubts and suspicions. The high rate of turnover is indicative of the disillusionment resulting from unrealistic expectations built up by corporate recruiters and the insignificant work assignments given young men on their first jobs.

Later in life, generally when they have married and their first child has reached the age of four or five, young parents will begin to feel economic pressures. These pressures will

Money will come easily.

cause some of them to conform more nearly to the older generation's demands, but the decision to conform will be difficult and soul-searching, because pride in their independence is deep-rooted and very real. To agree to become more dependent is contrary to their very real drive to become independent and assume responsibility.

AFTER TWENTY-FIVE

If it is true that young people may conform more easily later in life, it would seem logical to avoid hiring anyone under the age of twenty-five. This conclusion is especially appealing when one considers the studies which show the average college graduate will have three different jobs in his first five years out of school. Let someone else recruit, hire, train, and motivate the young nonconformist!

Unfortunately, there are two fallacies in this line of reasoning. First, we do not have the luxury of time to wait five years or more. Most major companies are already complaining of managerial shortages. Expansion of business is virtually impossible without new people, particularly those being groomed for future management. The second fallacy of letting someone else do the hiring is analogous to the case of the pretty old maid who waited too long for the perfect man to come along. The outstanding young men will be easily identified, wooed, and won early by competition. The promising young men will be cultivated and developed by the concerns that are involved with youth. Literally, there will be slim pickings left for the company that decides to let someone else hire the young nonconformist.

James L. Isham, president of the advertising agency Needham, Harper, and Steers, speaking to the Chicago Advertising Club recently stated: "The new breed of account executive will likely have been a student leader, articulate, highly motivated, successful in extracurricular activities—perhaps even a dissenter. The dissenter is, after all, a person who looks at old problems in new ways. We should welcome people who are inventive and dedicated and who have a passion for problem solving." [3]

POSITIVE MOTIVATORS

The young graduates today are motivated primarily toward serving all humanity and making the entire world a cleaner and safer place. Honesty to oneself and to others is more revered than blind obedience to dogma, putting something over on a competitor, or abusing the environment for a profit.

It is difficult for a veteran of the military service who is now an executive in business to understand the so-called anti-American behavior of some of the young extremists. Often the executive dismisses the problem because he feels it is only 1 or 2 percent of the college population that seeks mass publicity. He does not want to think about the majority that often not only tolerates but supports the minority.

Many books have been written in an attempt to redress

[3] "MBA no 'requirement for employment,'" *Marketing Insights,* Mar. 2, 1970, p. 1. Copyright 1970 by Crain Communications, Inc.

the abuses of the American Negroes, American Indians, Mexican Americans, Japanese Americans, and other minorities. Indeed, many executives and corporations have donated fortunes to assist these people. Through communications satellites and other modern mass communications media, underprivileged and abused people around the world have aroused the sympathy and empathy of our young college people.

Living in an affluent society, young people are not particularly sympathetic toward an old corporation which has exploited the natural resources of a poor foreign country without helping its citizens. When a minority on campus protests such treatment, the majority actually supports the cause. An unpopular United States government announcement or action is often criticized by the press and leaders of the opposition party as well as by business leaders. It should not surprise executives when their growing children also criticize their government or country. They are being taught to do so, objectively and intelligently.

FOREIGN COMPETITION AND EXECUTIVE SHORTAGES

Dun and Bradstreet, Inc., recently polled the 300 members of its President's Panel about the business problems of the next decade. They report that the overriding problem of the seventies will be foreign competition.[4]

Governments all over the world each day are establishing

[4] "Foreign Competition—Biggest Problem in the 1970s?" *Dun's Review*, December, 1969, p. 41.

new rules for business, creating whole new sets of problems. Multinational companies are being created through global expansion and mergers and acquisitions. Borrowing money abroad, national tariffs, and income taxes imposed on individuals and corporations are growing topics of concern.

One panelist, J. Peter Grace, president of W. R. Grace and Company, is quoted as follows:

> The competition for executives will continue to become more intense. Top managements will need to concern themselves more not just with maintaining morale, but more fundamentally, with creating an environment that satisfies the basic objectives of the executives coming up through the organization. The most important factor will be to satisfy the executive that his talents and skills are being more fully used. In many cases, this will involve more rapid promotion, and hence a degree of risk-taking, greater than that which many organizations have been willing to assume.[5]

Clearly, today's youth is more concerned with worldwide problems than prior generations were at the same age. Fortunately top management in business is becoming aware of the same problems today.

Finally, when corporate recruiters visit a campus, they literally woo the few seniors who are interested in a business career. Because of the shortage, the recruiters raise the starting salary and offer to outbid competition. The student is both embarrassed by and contemptuous of such tactics, although he will often take the highest offer because in his innocence he feels all companies are equally bad. Cocktail parties sponsored by recruiters are not uncommon, and dinner with drinks at an expensive restaurant is very common. The lavish sales pitch of the recruiter for his company

[5] *Ibid.*

builds up the student's expectation of a high salary and an opportunity for rapid advancement for the man who can achieve company goals. Money and discipline or pressure! If the recruiter hires a clean-shaven, well-dressed graduate who has only average grades, the better students may think less of the company. The student's clean image is often a facade to hide his contempt for the employer. Too many companies put their worst foot forward on campus and inadvertently perpetuate the myth that all business is selfish and unchallenging.

CONCLUSIONS

Today's college graduates include many good prospects for business and industry, men and women who someday will make excellent managers. They do not understand what business represents and do not recognize the truly satisfying feeling that can be obtained through doing the job.

This generation will not respond as desired to higher and higher salaries and traditional management practices of discipline and pressure. Its members are not particularly interested in helping business grow ever larger and perhaps more abusive. They are sincerely interested in helping *all* humanity and solving international problems. Top management is now beginning to think along similar lines as business grows in international dimensions. The attitudes of both generations will have to be modified through education and communication.

CHAPTER THREE

Resolving the Dilemma

IT IS GENERALLY AGREED that if business is to grow, we need these young college people now. If they won't respond to traditional management methods of money and discipline, then modern management methods must be used to obtain the energized and loyal employees whom management desires. Clearly, the students' neutral or hostile attitudes must be converted into positive attitudes. Because students may be naïve or confused, the burden of building positive motivation falls on existing business management.

EXISTING
POSITIVE MOTIVATION

Young college people today are strongly motivated. It is their desire to satisfy such inner needs as sincerity, honesty, and the unselfish serving of others which makes them act as they do. They also have a strong desire to find their individual places in life where they can serve both mankind and themselves. This desire is often expressed in their concern for self-development. They want to know what kind of training they will receive and into what areas the career path may take them.

Unfortunately, traditional managers interpret such concern as the case of an innocent youth wanting to be a vice-president without working for it. Since many young people feel lower-management-level jobs are routine and without challenge, they are concerned with how long it will take them to rise to a position where they can make decisions which will help their fellow men. They are willing to work, and work hard, for things in which they believe. If they are to work for business instead of merely tolerating it or working against it, they must be convinced that good business serves humanity.

Young college people are intelligent and socially sophisticated; hence they see through false and misleading business propaganda. It is a foolish waste of company resources to claim an industry does not pollute the air and the water if it really does. It is equally foolish to claim an industry is not exploiting a minority labor group or the physical re-

You want to be vice president?

sources of an area if it really does. Young people have seen such abuses, and they have studied documented case histories of exploitation. Mass communication has highlighted the bad and more often ignored, or certainly played down, the good. On the basis of news coverage, it is very easy to make the false generalization that most businesses are selfish and profit-oriented for the benefit of a few at the expense of the masses.

RESISTING CHANGE

It is necessary to understand how a young person thinks about change, and how he reacts to change, if we are to change *his* behavior. All organisms tend to maintain the constancy of the internal conditions essential to their well-being. For example, normal body temperature is 98.6°. If the body is too hot, we perspire and evaporation cools the body. If the body is too cold, we shiver and burn energy to warm up. The body also requires a given level of food, water, and rest. Once the normal balance is disturbed, automatic functions give rise to drives that stimulate us to restore the needed balance or constancy.

This concept has been found to apply also to the broad external relationships between a person and his social environment. When a danger or need is drawn to an individual's attention, a state of tension or restlessness will arise and persist until the need is satisfied or merged with another state, such as action. In business, a young person should be approached with the realization that normally he is happy with status quo and is likely to resist change. Change means uncertainty and is often seen as a threat. Resisting change serves to protect the young person from the manager who wishes to disturb his self-satisfied sense of well-being.

Once a young person is confronted with a situation involving change, such as graduation from college, he can no longer remain psychologically at rest and must act to restore his inner balance. Changing his sense of values is one way he can restore the inner balance. Thus at this transitional phase of his life, leaving school and going out into the unknown world, he is susceptible to a reassuring message.

THE BENEFITS OF BUSINESS

Today's young people can be persuaded that business does infinitely more good for the masses than it does harm. Millions of older citizens are living on funds invested in the stock of corporations, and without profit many of these retired people would be on welfare or relief rolls. It is common today for labor contracts to include guaranteed pensions, and most of the accumulated pension funds also are invested in business and finance. Thus it is to labor's advantage that our economy continue to profit and grow. For years many companies have made it a practice to hire the handicapped, and more companies are now giving special training to the disadvantaged. Without the assistance of business, these people would live without hope and perpetuate the ghettos. The cost of a college education, rising every year, is offset partially by profits from investment trusts which are owned by the colleges.

Many companies that offer tuition refund programs for employees have proved that the better-educated employee produces more, is generally more efficient, and is ultimately more loyal. Such programs begin at pre-high-school levels and continue through postgraduate work at the doctoral level. Many persons who delayed completing their education or could not seek a higher education earlier in life have benefited by such company programs. None of this could have happened without profit and the economics of a good return on invested capital.

Profitable operations create a demand for equipment and land, a demand for labor, a demand for training and the constant upgrading of skills and knowledge, a demand for buildings and office equipment, a demand for highly educated leadership. Competition requires a more efficient use of natural resources, buildings, and equipment as well as of people and their individual development. Competition also creates improvements in products, systems, and services while holding costs to a minimum. Indeed, after fifty years of struggling along, the U.S.S.R. has decided to put its manufacturing plants on a profit and loss basis as an incentive to good management. European and Asiatic countries are sending their best young men to American graduate business schools to learn modern management techniques. These countries are also attempting to hire American professors to build their own graduate business schools in the American image.

Business today has an enlightened self-interest. In other words, business has found it pays more to use natural resources, facilities, and people for their own benefit than it pays to exploit them. For example, in the paper industry trees are being grown faster than they are being cut down. More factories are fireproof and air-conditioned than ever before, and the typical modern plant is architecturally very attractive with the surrounding area well landscaped. Waste has been reworked to remove valuable chemicals and minerals which formerly polluted the air and water.

It is a fact, and we should admit it, that our air and

water are not as pure as they should be. What is not commonly understood is the fact that individual companies have spent hundreds of millions of dollars to purify waste. Many have achieved as high as 90 percent removal of impurities, but the remaining 10 percent is still a large and expensive problem. But any business problem represents a challenge!

CHALLENGING THE YOUNG GRADUATES

Perhaps these bright young college people can come up with better answers to solve such business problems for the good of all mankind and for their own selfish place in this world. Perhaps they can change the establishment for the better by increasing employment and creating more opportunities for all people to improve their lot in life. Perhaps they can develop better ways to reach and serve undeveloped countries and raise the standard of living around the world. Ultimately, they may find ways to reduce overpopulation, feed starving millions of people, and lessen the danger of nuclear and biological warfare. These problems are very real and truly represent a challenge to anyone. If our young college people can help solve such problems, they should be most welcome. They do have a sense of social and environmental responsibility which business strongly needs.

But what of the small concern which is barely surviving by manufacturing, for example, miniature flashlights or other simple products? Companies of this type also have the responsibility of providing employment for people. They have the responsibility of providing a base for the development of new markets and new products. They have the responsibility of considering those who may have invested their life savings in the hope of living a retired life on their own funds rather than on public welfare. The challenge to young people is equally large regardless of the size of a business or its products and services. This fact must be communicated to our college people in terms of *their* selfish interests.

TECHNIQUES OF
COMMUNICATING WITH YOUTH

In advertising one commonly sees communications which follow the tried and proved AIDA (attention, interest, desire, action) formula. An attention-getting picture, teaser, or heading captures the imagination of the target audience. In the body of the advertisement are facts and figures which describe the benefits to the user of the product or service. This approach builds interest and desire. Finally, a good ad concludes by asking for specific action: join the crusade, vote for this candidate, try this new product!

If the target has been well segmented out of the general population, the advertisement can use language which the chosen segment can understand and believe. Placed in the right media at the appropriate time and desired frequency, it will gain the desired exposure. Such an advertisement, well designed graphically and employing both logical and emotional appeals, will communicate and persuade. Basic techniques of this type can be used today to convert the hostile or neutral attitudes of youth into positive, friendly attitudes toward business.

As an example, late in 1969 the Equitable Life Assurance Society of New York, a company with a traditional conservative image, ran an advertisement in fifty-seven college newspapers. It was a picture of Albert Einstein with tousled long hair. The caption said: "Hair. It's not the style that counts, it's what's under it." The ad included an offer of a free 18- by 24-inch poster version, and within a week Equitable received 3,200 requests.[1]

The Bettmann Archive, Inc.

[1] Reprinted with permission from *Advertising Age*, Feb. 23, 1970, p. 2. Copyright 1970 by Crain Communications, Inc.

In addressing a group of college students today, Richard Borden's "ho-hum" formula for public speaking is still one of the best practical guides. He suggests an opening statement or question to wake up an audience. For example, "How many people will be born in India, starve in Africa, get sick in Japan, or die of an auto accident in the United States?" Dick Borden states that once the audience is awake, the speaker must then answer the unspoken question "Why bring that up?" In other words, "What has your opening shocker to do with me, the listener?" A transition might be as follows: "I state these facts because while you and I are well fed and healthy, others are in dire need of your support. My company wants to do more in the area of . . . ."

Wake them up!

Because of natural distrust or suspicion, Borden's next question from the listener is "For example?" An illustration of a speaker in tune with his listeners might be as follows: "In the Watts area of Los Angeles, for example, we spent several hundred thousand dollars training people to use electronic testing equipment to check our production of . . . ."

Finally, the last question in the mind of the listener in the Borden formula is "So what?" In other words, "Specifically what do you want me to do about it?" Should the listener simply think well of your company, or buy stock in your company, or join your company and develop some better solutions to your problems?

THE REALISTIC COMPANY RECRUITER

In a personal interview, a recruiter is literally selling the college youth, and he should at least be aware of some proved sales techniques. If the recruiter has listened to the applicant, he will know what "turns him on" or, generally, where the applicant's inner motivation lies. He can then whet the appetite of the youth by arousing his curiosity, stating his theme in terms the young man will understand and with which he is apt to agree. The recruiter can then go on to paint the picture of a particular place in life for the young man to help serve mankind now and to achieve his own self-fulfillment in the future. The company recruiter can adapt his presentation to the particular applicant at that instant in time, and he can answer questions and resolve doubts. He can then ask for a decision and gain a favorable action on the spot.

For example, a college recruiter for a paper company might listen to a young man describe his hobby of hunting, fishing, and camping in addition to his desire to be in advertising. The recruiter himself might introduce the problems all paper companies have in trying to reduce water and air pollution. He might ask if the youth would be willing to help the company with what it is doing to improve the pollution situation and to inform the public about its progress. Certainly the recruiter would also mention the company's reforestation program and the large number of acres of timber it raises, the stocked game, and the lakes filled with fish and reserved for campers. This approach is not talking down to the applicant or misleading him but merely adapting the message to the auditor in terms which he is apt to listen to, understand, and approve. The youth is much more apt to prefer this kind of recruiter to the typical man who talks in terms of tons of production and growth of profit. The typical college senior knows where to obtain financial and historical data on a company; thus a recruiter need not emphasize such topics. The interview should be an exchange of ideas and attitudes, which can then be used to motivate the applicant positively.

The particular technique used to communicate with and persuade young college people is not nearly as important as the feeling of empathy. Each of the techniques described above showed that the businessman was putting himself in the shoes of the young man, not necessarily agreeing with him but fully understanding the position as the youth saw it. This type of approach is fundamental in communicating with young people.

IMMATURITY

Chris Argyris's immaturity-maturity theory notes some of the changes which should take place in the personality of an individual as he develops and matures over the years.[2] An immature person is passive and relatively dependent on his superiors. As he learns and becomes experienced, he has increased activity and independence. An immature person in business will have only a few behavior patterns, and he will have erratic and shallow interests in life. A mature person in business is capable of behaving in many ways and has deeper and stronger interests in life. The immature person has a short time perspective; hence he is normally impatient, while the mature person has a long time perspective of both past and future which gives him wisdom. The immature person has little awareness of himself and often acts impulsively, while the mature person is more aware of himself and has greater control over his behavior. Young people need guidance to make some of these normal changes and so become productive in business, government, education, or organizations of any kind.

[2] Chris Argyris, *Interpersonal Competence and Organizational Effectiveness*, Dorsey, Homewood, Ill. 1962. See also Chris Argyris, *Integrating the Individual and the Organization*, Wiley, New York, 1964.

CONCLUSIONS

It is the responsibility of modern management to convert the neutral and hostile attitudes of youth into positive, constructive attitudes. Business has many good causes to be championed and benefits to humanity which must be made clear to young people.

Since only 1 in 100 college seniors now feels a business career offers him an opportunity to help others, many business problems may be presented as a challenge to youth to give others real help. Near graduation time, young people are very susceptible to such a message.

There are a number of proved techniques for communicating with people and persuading them. Advertising, public speaking, and salesmanship each have principles which can guide the process.

These fine young people honestly want to serve their fellow man, to grow and develop themselves at least to a position where they can influence company policy for the better. They want a challenge to solve problems which have not been solved by prior generations or to which more appropriate solutions can be found. Many of these young people need guided experiences to become mature and truly productive in our society.

Young college people today can become willing, contributing members of business if men in business do not force them away by thoughtless words and actions.

CHAPTER FOUR

Handling
the New Generation Now

HAVING GAMBLED AND HIRED ONE of these bright young men, what does management do with him? It takes special skills and training to handle the graduate so as not to damage him or wreck the organization. He may resent and will probably rebel against an autocratic leader who tells him exactly what he must do, and yet he is still wet behind the ears. Must he be babied and burped? Decidedly no!

These bright young adults, brought up in a permissive society, do respect many of their professors at college. They particularly like and will work hard for a friendly teacher, one who will take time to listen to their individual problems and advise them. They actually seek out the friendly authority who will permit admitting one's faults and fears without incurring a lecture. They want to level with someone who will guide them honestly and individually.

45

STYLES OF LEADERSHIP

Over the years Ohio State University has become famous for its studies of leadership behavior. Dr. Andrew W. Halpin conducted twelve studies involving groups of 1,065, 1,500, 2,361, and 2,000 subjects as diverse as aircraft commanders, factory foremen, school superintendents, management trainees, and business managers of a large oil company. The researchers questioned each leader's work group and his superiors on 1,790 items, reduced the list to 150 items, and then through factor analysis reduced the list to 40 items. For better understanding the results are clustered in two dimensions, as shown in Figure 4-1.

On the horizontal axis, "Initiating Structure in Interaction," the leader delineates relationships between himself and his group members. He establishes well-defined pat-

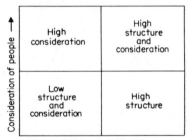

FIG. 4-1. The Ohio State leadership quadrants. (SOURCE: Paul Hersey and Kenneth H. Blanchard, *Management of Organizational Behavior,* Prentice-Hall, Englewood Cliffs, N.J., 1969.)

terns of organization, channels of communication, and ways of getting the job done. When a new problem arises, the group members are not dependent on the leader for instructions. On the vertical axis, "Consideration of People," the leader establishes friendships and mutual trust between members of the group and between the leader and his subordinates. There are respect and genuine warmth in all their relationships. Highly effective leaders, in all the diverse fields studied, not only scored high in both the two clusters, "Initiating Structure" and "Consideration," but scored well above their peer group.

THE MANAGERIAL GRID [1]

Robert Blake and Jane Mouton applied popular words to this Ohio State University concept to develop their Managerial Grid (see Figure 4-2). They use five leadership styles:

IMPOVERISHED: This style involves the exertion of the minimum effort to get required work done appropriate to sustain organization membership.

COUNTRY CLUB: Thoughtful attention to the needs of people for satisfying relationships leads to a comfortable, friendly organization atmosphere and work tempo.

TASK: Efficiency in operations results from arranging conditions of work in such a way that human elements interfere to a minimum degree.

[1] Robert R. Blake and Jane S. Mouton, *The Managerial Grid*, Gulf, Houston, 1964. See also Robert R. Blake et. al., "Breakthrough in Organization Development," *Harvard Business Review*, November–December, 1964, p. 136.

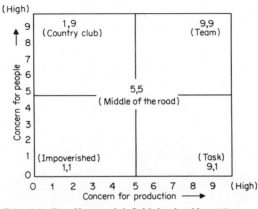

FIG. 4-2. The Managerial Grid leadership styles.
(SOURCE: Paul Hersey and Kenneth H. Blanchard, *Management of Organizational Behavior,* Prentice-Hall, Englewood Cliffs, N.J., 1969.)

MIDDLE OF THE ROAD: Adequate organization performance is possible through balancing the necessity to get out work with the maintenance of morale at a satisfactory level.

TEAM: Work accomplished is from committed people; interdependence through a common stake in the organization purpose leads to relationships of trust and respect.

Blake and Mouton added numerical scaling to the original concept; they stress a 9, 9, or team, approach to leadership rather than an extreme task orientation or an extreme concern for people. Such theories were very popular in the early 1960s.

Rensis Likert, an authority in this field, follows the same pattern.[2] The implication throughout Likert's writings is that the ideal and most productive leader behavior is em-

[2] Rensis Likert, *New Patterns of Management,* McGraw-Hill, New York, 1961. See also Rensis Likert, *The Human Organization,* McGraw-Hill, New York, 1967.

ployee-centered, or democratic. His own findings raise questions as to whether there can be a single style of leadership which can apply in all situations. For example, 4 of 12 leaders using the "ideal" type of leadership had low producing sections, and 1 of 10 supervisors using the "poor" type of leadership had a high producing section.

In disagreement is another authority, Saul W. Gellerman, who studied leadership behavior in a General Electric plant. He wrote:

> Place an individual with strong independence drives under a supervisor who needs to keep men under his thumb, and the result is very likely to be trouble. Similarly, if you take docile men who are accustomed to obedience and respect for their supervisors and place them under a supervisor who tries to make them manage their own work, they are likely to wonder uneasily whether he really knows what he is doing. . . . The lowest morale in the plant was found among those men whose foremen were rated *between* the democratic and authoritarian extremes. The G.E. research team felt that these foremen may have varied inconsistently in their tactics, permissive at one moment and hardfisted the next, in a way that left their men frustrated and unable to anticipate how they would be treated.[3]

More recently, Fred Fiedler reported that in more than fifty studies covering a span of fifteen years it was found that *both* directive, task-oriented leaders and nondirective, human relations–oriented leaders are successful under some conditions.[4] Leader effectiveness is a function of *matching* style to the situation.

[3] Saul W. Gellerman, *Motivation and Productivity*, American Management Association, New York, 1965, pp. 42–43.

[4] Fred E. Fiedler, *A Theory of Leadership Effectiveness*, McGraw-Hill, New York, 1967. See also John J. Morse and Jay W. Lorsch, "Beyond Theory Y," *Harvard Business Review*, May–June, 1970.

The following brief illustrations may show how various stereotyped leaders might operate:

> J. J. AUTOCRAT, SALES MANAGER: "We are starting a drive on selling systems. I need your help, and I'm going to get it! On every call you make for the next month, make sure you talk to the office manager and tell him about our alpha-numeric system. If he is not in when you call, make an appointment to call back, but make damn sure you see everyone on the list. I'll be reading every call report, and I want to see every office manager's reaction to our system. And don't make up stories! I know most of these people, and I'll probably phone a number of them after you call.
>
> "Don't waste a lot of time trying to sell other products in our line this month! Our largest profit item is this alpha-numeric system, and it will lead to additional sales later. The old man wants our branch profit up this month, and I intend to see that he gets it! Our system is the best one available, so don't come back asking for special deals or special prices.
>
> "Any questions? If not, get off your tails and let's get those orders rolling in here!"

Given this type of direction, the men will move to keep their jobs, but they will not be motivated. The better salesmen will probably leave, and the mediocre men, who can't get other jobs, will stay. As the total group performance becomes lower, the autocratic leader will yell louder and become still more demanding.

> JOHN G. DEMOCRATIC, SALES MANAGER: "I've called you men together this morning because, as you know, our branch profit picture has been poor lately. What can we do about it?"
>
> FIRST SALESMAN: "Let's have a contest—you know, double commission after selling 100 percent of quota!"

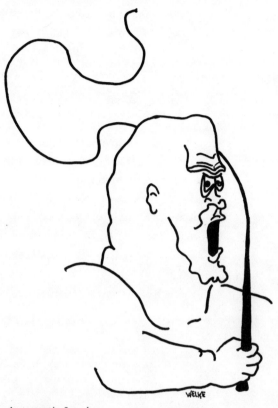

Autocratic Leader.

SECOND SALESMAN: "No, that'll never work. What we need is a lower selling price. Our systems are at least 20 percent higher than those of the competition."

SALES MANAGER: "Joe, what do you think we can do to improve our profit picture?"

THIRD SALESMAN: "Well, if we all push the new alpha-numeric system, we should get a short-term jump in profit, and it does seem superior to our competition."

FIRST SALESMAN: "I'll go for that if you throw in a contest!"

SALES MANAGER: "You know we can't change the compensation system. I suppose we could spring dinner for the top man and his wife at the end of the month. How does that sound, O.K.?"

SECOND SALESMAN: "I still don't like it, but since the others outvoted me, I'll go along with it."

A democratic leader depends upon the experience and judgment of the group. He runs the risk of having the group make a decision contrary to his own beliefs. His success is in direct proportion to the true wisdom of the subordinates. Many inexperienced or young people are frequently frustrated by this lack of direction. When decisions must be made quickly, the democratic process breaks down. Too often the system evolves into mediocre compromises between alternatives.

L. K. PATER, VICE-PRESIDENT, SALES: "Now, boys, we have a job to do, and I know you will help. Our branch profit is down a little, so we need a short-term push while we are waiting for some of these big quotations to become orders.

"Now, I've tried many different things in my twenty years of selling our products, and I know if we need short-term profits, the best product is our alpha-numeric system. It doesn't take long to sell, and it has a high profit margin."

FIRST SALESMAN: "But gee, L. K., you don't expect us to waste time calling on small accounts to sell the system and ignore the big quotes that are almost due to come in, do you?"

VICE-PRESIDENT, SALES: "Now, George, you know me better than that. I know you have to keep in close touch with your promising big deals, and I also know that for a short

time we can all make a few extra calls each day and bring
in those system orders. Believe me, I have risen to vice-
president by pleasing the old man this way. You take my
advice, and I'm sure every one of you will be successful
with this company."

Friendly Authority.

In modern business, this type of leader is often disguised as the friendly big brother rather than the omnipotent father. A bright young vice-president builds a personal following, and workers strive to be identified with his team. They will rarely suggest doing things differently even when they should. Subordinates hope to ride to success on the leader's coattails, but their loyalty blinds the leader to obvious pitfalls.

s. w. CONSULTATIVE, VICE-PRESIDENT, SALES: "Gentlemen, we have an edict from the old man: improve branch profits this month. You all know the alpha-numeric system has the largest gross profit, but what I want to know from you is how pushing this system will affect your other business?" First salesman: "Well, if we push a small-ticket item, we may improve profit, but our total sales volume will be a lot lower." Second Salesman: "Suppose we offer a special price deal this month only and sell the system like hot cakes?"

VICE-PRESIDENT, SALES: "No, gentlemen; no price deals. I'll decide what to do and take the responsibility for it, but no price deals. What other suggestions have you?"

THIRD SALESMAN: "The only way we can generate a high volume of systems orders would be to sell to national accounts with many locations that can all use it. But we can't neglect our other quotations that are pending."

FOURTH SALESMAN: "Well, we could all push harder for one month, I guess, but what's in it for us? I mean if branch profit goes up, how do we benefit?"

VICE-PRESIDENT, SALES: "Well, it seems to me you gentlemen agree the systems can be sold if we all push for one month. The danger is that we might neglect our other business. And Al thinks you all ought to share in the success. Now is there anything else I should consider before making the decision? Well then, here is what we will do. Each of you pick ten large accounts that can use the system in many locations. I'll make the calls with each of you, but we won't have the usual split-commission deal. You will receive 100 percent. That way you will still be able to cover your regular business and share in any boost in profits. Get me the names by the end of today, and we'll get started!"

The consultative leader seeks out the ideas and suggestions of his workers. He attempts to discover the advantages and disadvantages of alternative courses of action, but he reserves the power of decision to himself. Clearly, his success is a direct reflection of the advice he receives and the persuasive ability of the various subordinates he consults. His choice of subordinates is paramount to his effectiveness, either good or bad.

JAMES SUBSTANTIVE, VICE-PRESIDENT, SALES: "All right, gentlemen. You have all seen a copy of the old man's directive to me about improving profits. I've asked each of you to come prepared with your individual plans. Joe, what do you plan to do?"

FIRST SALESMAN: "Well, Jim, I've just completed my analysis of each account, and I can see about twenty-eight accounts give me almost 80 percent of my business while seventy or eighty accounts yield only 20 per cent. What I have decided to do is concentrate on the twenty-eight good ones and a very few potentially good accounts. I'm sure I can increase business and reduce my travel expenses considerably."

SECOND SALESMAN: "As you know, Jim, I sell only to national accounts, so I've decided to push our alpha-numeric system for multiple installations in each account. This will make additional contacts and friends in each account and will pay in bigger sales of our regular products in the future."

THIRD SALESMAN: "Jim, I'm going to need some help from you. Being relatively new in my territory, I don't know some of those people as well as I should. I'd like you to make joint calls with me on about ten large accounts that look promising. That should help me carry my share of the load."

VICE-PRESIDENT, SALES: "All right, men. Your plans look great. Of course I'll help you, Pete. You pick the accounts and set up the appointments. Just tell me what product or system they can use, and I'll be glad to cooperate. Gentlemen, if you will post me once a week, I'll be able to keep the old man happy and spend most of my time in planning our marketing strategy for next year to avoid seasonal situations like this."

The substantive leader must have complete faith in his subordinates' ability and willingness to accomplish the desired goals. The task or substance literally leads members of the group to perform their respective specialties. For example, the head of data-processing equipment is expected to be willing and able to implement systems which will help achieve the organization's goals. His superior, the substantive leader, is then free to work on long-range planning. Also essential under this style of leadership is a reporting and control system so that each member understands what all the others are doing and all members can go the same way.

ART MANIPULATIVE, VICE-PRESIDENT, SALES: "Charlie, I asked you to come in early so we could talk before the others get here. The old man wants our branch to raise its contribution to profits, and I figure our alpha-numeric system is the quickest way. You are my key salesman, Charlie; what do you think?"

CHARLIE: "Well, I don't know, Art. It takes a lot of time to sell that system, and I'd hate to let my other business slide. I guess it could be done, but you are asking a lot."

ART: "You plan to take your family to Mexico next fall, Charlie. Suppose I give you an extra week off (unofficially, that is); would that justify the extra push we need now?"

CHARLIE: "Say, that's great, Art. Thanks! And I've got an idea how you might get Pete to go along with us. He is buying a new sports car and would probably welcome a chance to pick up some extra expense account money."

ART: "I see. You think if I assign some distant accounts to Pete, he'll push hard to justify his expenses. That's not a bad idea. But what about Bill? What makes him tick?"

CHARLIE: "Bill has been bragging a lot lately about his sales ability. Why not start a simple contest, say, dinner for two? You know Bill. He'll break his back for a month just to be on top."

ART: "O.K., Charlie. When the men come in later, I want you to talk it up enthusiastically so they all get into the spirit of the thing."

Knowing the boss is a manipulator, the men automatically resist his propositions until he gives them something extra. From experience they learn to bargain with him, and they give him only enough to fulfill their share of the bargain and no more. The job itself is still work with little or no pleasure. For a short term, with some people, this kind of leadership can be very effective, but in the long run it does not motivate people to grow and develop so they can contribute substantially more to the organization.

The management style which a man exhibits in a given situation may often reflect a total organization's attitude. In a dynamic, risk-taking company, for example, swift action and continued change are expected. Conversely, in an old, traditional industry seeking mere survival, the prevalent attitude is not to rock the boat with anything new or different.

Regardless of the system of classification of styles of leadership, the studies consistently show that most managers have a *single* style of leadership. Their behavior pattern is the same whether their followers are young or old, experienced or neophytes, knowledgeable or untrained! The pattern remains the same without regard to the time element or the myriad of variables in different situations. For example, W. J. Reddin reports that about 70 percent of the managers whom he tested have a single dominant style and a single supporting style.[5] Only 6 percent of the managers used three or more styles of leadership!

Clearly, there are times when direct commands are essential and an autocratic leader is desirable. Some employees may need friendly encouragement to build their confidence, while others, at the same time, may need a firm leader who will not tolerate poor performance on critical tasks. Obviously there are times when a compromise is indicated to maintain group cooperation and teamwork. On occasion, harmony and friendly relationships are essential to success. On other occasions it might be appropriate for a boss to stay out of the way and let his subordinates sink or swim on

[5] W. J. Reddin, *Management Style Diagnosis Test: Test Interpretation Manual,* Fredericton, N.B., 1965.

their own. To maximize the efforts of subordinates effectively in both short- and long-run tasks, the modern executive *changes* his style of leadership as appropriate to the total situation at a given point in time, and he motivates people *individually*, changing his style to match their needs or problems.

On occasion, a group of experienced subordinates must be sold on a proposal before they will cooperate as desired. If the selling is done openly and honestly, it might be called leading by persuasion. If it is done on the strength of the leader's personality, it might be called leading by charisma. If it is done by devious means, such as promising rewards to selected subordinates, it might be called leading by manipulation or implicit bargaining. Since people normally resist change, an autocratic leader who tells subordinates what they must do simply aggravates the situation. A democratic leader attempting to change a system runs the risk of being outvoted. Clearly, a knowledge of the psychology of communication and persuasion is desirable under conditions of change.

An effective leader normally is flexible in his use of styles of leadership. As the experience level of subordinates varies and as situations vary, so should the leadership. On occasion, because of either time or distance, a decision must be made without consulting expert subordinates. How this decision is communicated to subordinates can very well mean the difference between full cooperation and sullen behavior. Frustrated subordinates will often sabotage a program without violating a letter of their instructions.

Young people will respond as desired to an appropriate

style of leadership, and the manager *should change* his style of leadership as the variables dictate. Consistency in exhibiting the same style of leadership under all conditions dooms a manager to failure in developing young people.

FRIENDLY AUTHORITY

The modern manager looks and acts like a friendly authority who is interested in the development of the young employee. The manager encourages the neophyte to talk freely of his ambitions, his strengths, and his weaknesses. He listens for clues to the subordinate's existing motivation, searching for discrepancies between what is and what might be. While it is relatively easy to generalize about any group, it is more difficult to isolate the key characteristics which differentiate the individual. What level does the subordinate aspire to reach at this early stage of his career? Is he motivated by status, prestige, recognition, challenge, team association, self-development, serving others, or something else?

Given some clues to what the individual and unique subordinate wants, the manager asks where the subordinate is most apt to receive the kind of reward he seeks. For example, will the subordinate benefit more by working for an outspoken, gregarious supervisor or by working for a quiet and demanding supervisor? We can teach young people that there are a predetermined route and pace to success which do not demand all their energy if they do not rock the boat with new ideas. Reinforcing this kind of behavior breeds mediocrity or discontent in the future. On the other hand, if a supervisor learns of the individual differences between college graduates assigned to him and then treats each man according to his particular needs, he can design meaningful work for each of the new people. Since the young man is bright, the initial assignment should be challenging to his intelligence and demanding of his energies. Selecting the appropriate area for initial placement can make a tremendous difference in the subsequent turnover of young employees.

MANAGEMENT BY EXCEPTION

Once the new man has learned the job requirements, which will probably take less time than older generations took, and he is ready to solo, he should be given an area of authority to do the job and a responsibility to report its progress. While he should know what the goals and objectives are, he should be left to his own devices to reach these goals. This approach will give him an opportunity for achievement, responsibility, recognition, personal growth, and an interest in the work itself. These are Fred Herzberg's positive motivators to utilize human potential more effectively by designing work so that it causes people to grow and develop rather than wither and stagnate.

Instead of employing traditional "management by objectives" as normally abused in practice, with constant pressure and ulcer-producing needling or other help from Big Brother, the manager should leave the young subordinate on his own. This is the modern management concept of "management by exception." [6]

In management by exception the subordinate is given an area in which to operate and for which he alone is responsible. Within that area he is not only permitted but forced to operate his own way without interference. The superior gets routine reports of performance and progress, but he stays out of the way. Only when something comes along that is outside the area of delegated responsibility does the young subordinate go to his boss. In other words, only the exceptions are triggered to the attention of the boss; all routine items are left to the young man to do in his own way. Not incidentally, his way may be different and on occasion very much better than the supervisor's way. The point is simply that within his area the young man is important, needed, and trusted to do his best for the good of all.

One apparent disadvantage of applying this concept is that it places the manager in the role of an error-detecting servomechanism. "It is rough on the manager, for he receives nothing but bad news all day. If things are going right, he gets no signals; all he hears about are deviations from what is supposed to be happening." [7]

When the concept is applied appropriately, the manager does get progress reports which are favorable. He has time to observe the personal development of his young subordi-

[6] Lester R. Bittel, *Management by Exception,* McGraw-Hill, New York, 1964.

[7] Myron Tribus, as quoted in "The Management Machine—Can It Work?" *Dun's Review,* vol. 94, no. 6, p. 27, December, 1969.

nates. When asked for a report by top executives, the manager has the opportunity to show off his promising subordinates by bringing them into the conference. These are a few of the deep personal satisfactions that a manager does achieve on the job. His relief from routine processing also gives him much-needed time for long-range planning.

JOB ENLARGEMENT

As soon as the young man proves his ability in the limited area of delegated responsibility, the job should be broadened to ensure a growth and development process. For example, a six-month apprenticeship established in 1950 may be ridiculous twenty years later for today's college people. Time should be related to performance today, not to past experience with a slower generation operating under different economic conditions. If we are to train young people properly, we must use caution in reinforcing the desired behavior so as to avoid maintaining the comfortable status quo.

The broadened job assignment should have the limits of authority clearly spelled out and the reporting-back function understood. Once again the supervisor keeps his hands off and permits the young man to operate in his own way. Only when something occurs which is outside the area of the young man's responsibility does he seek the assistance of his superior.

The job can be broadened as rapidly as the young man proves capable of handling it. With periodic performance appraisals, the manager can point out strengths and weaknesses in an acceptable climate of trust and growth. As the friendly authority, the manager can suggest changes, improvements, or self-development activities which the young man eagerly wants and needs. The manager can also listen for clues which indicate a raising of the young man's level of aspiration or a change in his interests and self-motivation.

PARTICIPATION IN DECISION MAKING

Modern management practice also encourages suggestions from subordinates in the decision-making process. Traditional managers resent the newcomer's attempting to change anything. They reason that if the old way was good enough to earn X amount of profit, it should be left alone. Unfortunately, the old way may have prevented the company from earning two or three times X profit. Or new conditions, new tools, new systems, or new people may enable a change to benefit the company.

Computer-minded young executives are disrupting the traditional organization charts to fit the style of new management and to meet the demands of industry and a changing environment. Management science, operations research, cybernetic decision making, and other modern management tools permit greater flexibility in running a business. Modern management in the 1970s will be made up of men who are comfortable in the presence of risk and who also have a high tolerance for ambiguity and uncertainty.

In this age of conglomerates and mergers, some corporations make a practice of spinning off divisions to form separate operating divisions. They feel this practice gives young managers a chance to show what they can do. It was recently reported in the business press: "Many of the widely touted old management maxims are crumbling too, such as the notion that a man should report to only one boss. Today, with the emphasis on task forces and project teams, a mid-level executive or staff man may find himself checking in with half a dozen bosses." [8]

The results of many research studies show that the more suggestions accepted by top management, the greater the productivity, efficiency, and morale. This rule also holds true when subordinates have the feeling they can at least influence the decisions made by their bosses. They know the modern manager will listen to their viewpoints.

LEVEL OF EXPECTATION

Most young college people will move to meet the level expected of them by their professors. If the teacher accepts poorly researched and poorly written papers and then grades on a curve, the class soon performs at that level. They meet his level of expectation. On the other hand, if he states his higher expectations and rejects anything below that level, the young people check their research data, use the dictionary, and really do rise to meet the professor's level of expectation.

[8] "The New Management Finally Takes Over," *Business Week,* Aug. 23, 1969, p. 58.

In business, traditional management expects the worst of the neophyte and he meets that level of expectation. Modern managers demand a high level of performance, and today's young graduates respect that demand and rise to meet it. Given the authority to act for their department and the manager's expectations that they will perform at a superior level, these young people will produce at the manager's high level of expectation.

For example, one man may perform marginally and with little interest in one department, then suddenly blossom out when transferred to another department doing similar work. Too often, traditional management assumes the man suddenly changed, matured, or possibly had additional family responsibility thrust upon him. What is overlooked by traditional management and is sought by modern management is the effect of the different levels of expectation of the two immediate superiors involved. College students today respond readily to an authority's level of expectation, and they will do so tomorrow in business. It is the manager's option to expect mediocrity or to expect superiority. His attitude is generally quite easily understood and greatly influences the results he gets in return.

CONCLUSIONS

Modern management dictates that the young men in the new generation be handled as unique individuals. The modern manager will make it his business to know what each young man wants to do now and what he aspires to be in the future. He will select an appropriate initial assignment and placement with a friendly authority to guide the youngster's growth and development honestly.

The modern manager uses the concept of management by exception, narrowly at first but broadening as fast as the subordinate proves his ability and indicates a desire for greater authority and willingness to accept responsibility for his performance. The bright young man is encouraged to suggest different and better ways to accomplish a desired goal. He is encouraged to participate in the decision-making process. By doing so, he becomes part of a better team and gains respect and recognition.

Finally, the modern manager is fully aware of the effect his level of expectation has on young people. He knows they will fall to mediocrity or worse if that is what he expects and permits. He also knows they will rise to superiority if that is what he expects and demands. College students do this in school today, and they are preconditioned to do it tomorrow in business.

CHAPTER FIVE

Identifying
the Potential Leaders

HAVING HIRED A NUMBER of bright young men and brought them along in their jobs to the point where they produce satisfactorily without close supervision, management is next faced with the problem of attempting to identify its future leaders.

In the past, management could afford the test of time to see who would survive various trials and pressures. After ten years, most companies would lose a number of impatient men; some men would not exhibit the proper company attitude or loyalty; and some men would prove they were not able to handle more complicated assignments. In the process, perhaps 90 percent of management candidates would be washed out, leaving only a handful of men for future management.

Today, with an existing shortage of more than 200,000 managers, business cannot afford the luxury of time, and the situation will worsen through the next decade. Business needs new people today, and, perhaps more critically, business needs good *managers* to fill today's manpower shortages. Tomorrow the shortage of middle-age managers will actually stifle a company's growth unless business identifies, trains, and promotes many of the young college people now entering business.

Just as in older generations, many of the youngsters today are "loners" and would be happy to remain that way. As a group, they do like the occasional spotlight of recognition but honestly do not seek the control and direction of others. The majority will be content if they have the respect of their fellow workers and superiors, a reasonable amount of job security, recognition, and modest job advancement in due time. Primarily, they want to become part of an organization that is helping all mankind. The majority of today's youngsters will be content if they feel their job in business is mentally and emotionally challenging. Leaders are the exception.

RESPONSIBILITY

A manager's decision on personnel often makes the difference between success and failure in having a job done correctly. When we are wrong in our judgment of other people on the job, our mistakes can reflect on us, our unit, or our company. Our mistakes can hurt us as well as the candi-

SIGNORE

Recognize the future leader?

dates hired. This is more apparent as we *promote* people to jobs with greater responsibility. A manager is judged, in large part, on the people he develops and promotes. Proper selection of people is a key activity in management, and it is the responsibility of line management, not the personnel staff.

Line managers should improve their ability to analyze and judge the personality, intelligence, and abilities of another person. There are tools which will permit better predictions of what a man is apt to do in a given set of circumstances. The objective is to minimize the bad risks and increase the number of promotable young people.

HIERARCHY OF NEEDS

One of the best ways to understand a person's motivation and his inner needs is Maslow's concept of a hierarchy of needs.[1] In this theory, there are five levels of needs which people strive to satisfy, and each level must be satisfied to some degree before a person will turn his attention to another level. The primary level encompasses man's basic, or physiological, needs such as food, clothing, shelter, and sleep. These needs are very short-term. Man eats, and he must eat again very quickly. Man breathes, and he must breathe again very quickly.

The next level is that of security or safety needs. Man wants to be free of physical danger; he wants to know he can afford food, clothing, and shelter next month and next year. He wants to feel he will not be deprived of his physiological needs in the future. He wants job security or a feeling that his skill is easily transferred to another job in the future.

After man has satisfied to some degree the first two needs, he then becomes aware of his next need, to affiliate with other people. Man normally enjoys being with other people. He wants to be accepted by a group—by his fellow workers, by his neighbors, by his friends and family. In other words, man has social needs of which he becomes aware after his physiological and security needs have been relatively well satisfied. Group norms tend to establish acceptable standards of behavior, and man needs to be accepted.

In the United States today the majority of people have more or less satisfied these three needs, and many are con-

[1] Abraham H. Maslow, *Motivation and Personality*, Harper, New York, 1954. See also Abraham H. Maslow, *Eupsychian Management*, Dorsey, Homewood, Ill., 1965.

tent at this level. They do not want to pay the price of seeking more out of life, or they do not aspire to achieve a higher level or a higher quality of life. It is those who do seek or need something more from among whom future leaders can be identified.

The fourth level in Maslow's theory is that of esteem, both self-esteem and recognition from others. Self-esteem is essential to self-confidence and maturity. This leads to prestige, and it also increases the desire for exercising power and control of others rather than being directed oneself. One begins to feel that he is useful and has some effect on his environment. Men seeking this level of need can make excellent managers in the future. They have the inner motivation to learn new skills and new knowledge as well as the drive or determination to influence their careers upward.

The highest level in Maslow's hierarchy of needs is that of self-actualization, or the need to maximize one's potential. This is what causes a man to practice many hours each day to become a concert pianist, a brain surgeon, a professional athlete, a financier, a captain of industry, or whatever he feels he must be. This man feels he has some control over physical and social factors, and he does not wait for things to happen but manipulates his environment to make them happen. This man is competent in his field, and he knows it. He has a compulsion to accomplish a task, and although he does not reject rewards, they are valuable to him in passing to assess his progress compared with that of other people. He needs concrete feedback about his work and success. Because of his high task orientation, however, he is not necessarily a good manager. His high degree of independence should be balanced by an understanding of the need for teamwork in business.

THE CHARISMATIC LEADER

The charismatic leader is most easily identified in business. He is the person who is capable of eliciting popular support in human affairs. Due to a strong personality, he assumes leadership and permits his followers to identify with him and to copy his values and behavior. He is the knowledgeable and courageous individual who takes charge when others hesitate. He has a strong inner need for leadership or the need to direct others. It is very important for this kind of person to be looked up to and to gain acceptance for his position from others.

This strong leader has a special need for rapid personal advancement through promotion. While he must have the respect of his subordinates, which he is fully capable of earning, he is primarily motivated to earn the respect of high authority. He expects guidance from his supervisors and training to do a better job. Given guidance and training, his inner motivation will compel him to assume responsibility as fast as situations and his superiors permit.

SUPERIOR PERFORMERS

A much larger group of potential leaders is found among those who evidence job satisfaction or those who enjoy doing their work and feel it is important to do a good job. They will voluntarily enlarge their job and take on more work. They learn how others do their jobs and how the pieces all fit together. They enjoy the social satisfaction of working as part of a team of superior people. Insofar as possible, they feel that they are their own bosses and that their superior is simply there to help them.

Because people in this group work well, independently of immediate supervision, they are often overlooked as potential leaders. A selfish manager can easily bypass the good, steady, quiet worker because this subordinate does not demand public recognition for his efforts. He may not be known outside his immediate work group. But this man does have potential. He is dedicated, loyal, and trainable. His potential can be converted into reality for the benefit of all. He is not compelled to lead others and wield power, but he can be taught to do a superior job in supervising others.

THE TROUBLEMAKERS

A third group of potential leaders consists of the outspoken troublemakers. Here the generation gap, or communications gap, becomes overwhelming, and understanding is lost to violent emotional stress. A bright youngster resents an authoritarian parent or boss, and he may use many tactics to thwart his intentions. He will take instructions literally and do precisely what he is told, knowing full well the meaning was quite different. After being reprimanded, he will subsequently question the simplest instructions, driving his superior to drink.

Being energetic, he will use his physical drive to move and stack things which should not be moved. He will invent dangerous games which may endanger the safety of others. He may go out of his way to violate posted rules and regulations to show his contempt for authority. Most often he will be outstandingly vocal in his protests against management and its methods.

Is this man a brat who needs a good spanking, or is he a potential leader? Assuming management recruited and hired a bright, healthy young man, then one must consider the probability that this troublemaker is simply bored and frustrated. His behavior often indicates intelligence, creativity, initiative, and, most important, leadership. It may take more patience and understanding to develop this young troublemaker into a positive and productive leader, but the rewards are well worth the effort.

Law enforcement people working in ghettos as well as national sales managers have frequently reported the "miraculous conversion" of notorious troublemakers into honest leaders. Many a promising labor union leader, potentially trouble for management, has been promoted satisfactorily into a supervisor's job. In each case, the man was singled out for recognition and given authority to act and a challenge to his leadership ability. Many times the intelligent young man is no longer bored and frustrated. Put on the management team, he changes his perspective and matures into a strong, positive leader.

MATCHING JOB DESCRIPTION
AND MANPOWER SPECIFICATION

Fundamental to predicting an individual's performance in a management job are the personnel tools of job description and manpower specification. The former describes the work to be done and the working relationship with others, internally and externally. The manpower specification, on the other hand, details the *minimum* and acceptable range of age, experience, education, and physical and personality traits required for any man to perform the job described.

The job description itemizes the major duties, authority, and responsibilities of the position as well as a brief description of the number and titles of subordinates; travel requirements; and key internal and external relationships. For example, a district sales manager's job description might read as follows:

DISTRICT SALES MANAGERS JOB DESCRIPTION

MAJOR DUTIES AND RESPONSIBILITIES
1. Staff and train salesmen and clerical employees in a branch sales office.
2. Supervise and direct the setting of quotas and the meeting of sales objectives.
3. Obtain market research information on customer needs, product applications, and competitive actions.
4. Conduct performance appraisal interviews with every subordinate semiannually and recommend salary action.
5. Conduct monthly sales meetings to motivate and educate the sales force.

6. Report monthly on progress in each of the above items to the national vice-president of sales.

SUPERVISES   Three experienced salesmen, two sales trainees, one senior account representative, one inside sales service man, and two secretaries.

TRAVEL REQUIREMENTS   Auto travel daily; away from home an average of one evening per week and one weekend per month.

KEY INTERNAL RELATIONSHIPS   Must cooperate almost daily with manager of production scheduling and at least weekly with vice-president of sales; must spend at least two days per month with each salesman.

KEY EXTERNAL RELATIONSHIPS   Must maintain friendly personal relationships with every major account ($500,000 per year) in his district; as manpower requirements dictate, must maintain recruiting contacts with local college personnel.

This example is obviously oversimplified in order to clarify the point: a job description does *not* indicate what kind of person might fill the job. It merely describes the work to be done and the appropriate policy, responsibilities, and authority of the job.

The manpower specification, on the other hand, states the *minimum* personnel requirement and indicates a range of acceptability or other desired attributes of the person who may fill the job. Normally, the manpower specification states minimum age permitted, education at a minimum level and a desired higher level, experience required as a prerequisite to being considered, and desired broader experience if available. The manpower specification should include any health or safety details appropriate, such as good eyesight, physical ability to carry samples, possession of a driver's license, acceptable physical appearance, and so forth. Finally, the manpower specification should indicate personality traits required, i.e., ability to meet and become friendly with strangers, ability to think on one's feet, ability to make fair and reasonable adjustments in the customer's office, ability to earn the respect of subordinates, and so forth.

The more detailed each of these two tools, the more valid they become in matching potential leaders properly to challenging opportunities. If the young candidate meets most or all of the required manpower specifications and he also meets several of the desired levels, one can more accurately predict his chances of success. If he is weak in one or two areas but is nevertheless the best available candidate, one can counsel the young man and guide his self-development in these weaker areas. Obviously, if he is overqualified, one can point this fact out objectively and avoid having a frustrated or hostile subordinate who might not understand why he had been passed over.

INTERVIEWING

If the line manager has written a job description and a manpower specification to fill the job, then others can assist in screening applicants. Often multiple interviews will yield a consensus which is more valid than one man's opinion. Persons doing the interviewing should be coached in questioning techniques and have realistic expectations rather

Judging the individual correctly.

than waste time eliciting information previously recorded.

Obviously an interview is the only direct method of evaluating the candidate's appearance, manner, and speech characteristics. It is a method of measuring quickness of oral response, persuasiveness, quality of oral expression, and reaction to unanticipated questions. An interview may furnish an estimate of the personal values, attitudes, and physical vigor needed for a particular job. An interview is essential if one is to tie together the bits of information obtained from all other sources and resolve any contradictory or misinformation.

If the job description includes operating under stress, then an interview can be conducted intentionally to put the candidate under stress without preparation or immediate help. The resultant behavior should be indicative of what might be expected in a real job situation.

Finally, a good interview provides the candidate with information regarding the job which can help him decide better whether he can fit into the situation. The candidate should conclude from his total interviewing experience that he has had a fair chance to present his qualifications. Whether promoted or not, the young man should have this feeling of fair treatment because it is essential for good morale.

The modern manager looks for consistent behavior patterns of past performance because this information has the highest predictive value in attempting to forecast future performance. How hard did the young man try to achieve what he states he wanted? What motivated him to achieve? These are the realistic questions which are rarely answered in written form but which can be developed in a two-way interview.

In a patterned interview, a manager asks a series of questions which are printed out in sequence, and he need not give much thought to preparing for the interview. Commercial lists are available, and the manager simply checks the response or makes minimal notes about the reply.

On the other hand, experienced managers prefer a dynamic interview. The interaction between the manager and the interviewee is real, alive, and dynamic. One way to find out what a young man really likes or dislikes is to draw him out of his protective shell by *asking questions without cueing the answers.* Otherwise he will say what he thinks the manager wants to hear and not what his real ideas, in-

terests, and attitudes may be. Direct questions often produce little but an obvious response. Indirect questions that
are not leading and cannot be answered by a yes or no or
a brief statement are generally more productive of information.

EXAMPLES OF DRAWING
OUT A YOUNG MAN

1. *Open-ended Questions:*
   "What kind of supervision would bring out the best in
      you?"
   "What would you consider preferred working condi-
      tions?"
   "How do you think a sales supervisor should treat
      you?"
   "What aspects of your life do you think are most im-
      portant?"
   "What are the characteristics of a good supervisor?"
   "How do you see yourself in this company in five
      years?"

2. *Problem-solving Questions:*
   "What would you do if you were asked to work late
      and you had an appointment?"
   "What would you say if your supervisor told you to do
      something one way and you thought you knew a
      better way?"
   "What would you do if you felt your manager was
      blaming you for something which could not have
      been avoided?"
   "What would you say if your manager told you to do
      something which you thought was wrong?"

"What would you do if you felt your manager was not taking enough time to explain things to you?"

3. *Once a manager has a young man opened up, he can keep the conversation going with the techniques of reflection and interpretation:*
   YOUTH: "I had some bad luck on my last assignment and decided to switch."
   MANAGER: "Bad luck?"
   YOUTH: "I wasn't really happy on that assignment."
   MANAGER: "You didn't think you were getting anywhere?"

   *While a reflective question simply restates part of what the young man said, an interpretive question is an attempt to state the meaning of what was said. For ex-*ample:
   YOUTH: "If I don't have a sales manager watching my every move, I can do much better."
   MANAGER: "You feel that close supervision impairs your ability to do a good job?"
   (or)
   "You resent your manager checking details?"
   (or)
   "You don't like anyone telling you what to do?"
   YOUTH: "I haven't missed a quota for a long time."
   MANAGER (intentionally misinterpreting): "You mean you just make quota on a regular basis?"

4. *Projective Questions. Phrase the question so that the young man must answer what he thinks other people believe or do. He will most often project his own ideas, attitudes, or opinions onto the third party. For* example:
   MANAGER: "What do you think most young men find the hardest part of their job?"

"What did most of the neighbors think of that part of town?"

"What do you think most young men rate highest in satisfaction on the job?"

"Do you think most married couples decide jointly about job changes?"

"Do you think most young men are good at handling many details at once?"

5. *Elaborative Questions:*

"I'm not sure I understand (follow you). Would you explain further?"

"That's very interesting; go on."

"Could you illustrate that to make it clearer for me?"

"What do you mean, fair (satisfactory, progress, etc.)?"

"How did that work (occur, come about)?"

"Why do you suppose he (they) reacted that way?"

CONCLUSIONS

Once a young man is identified as a potential leader, he should be given opportunities to prove his value and to develop his latent abilities. Using the job description and manpower specification documents, an older manager can guide the rapid career development of his bright young subordinate. If the youngster can be shown what higher jobs demand in the way of performance and preparation, he may very well take on additional training and rotating or temporary job assignments in order to achieve his individual goals eventually. Conversely, he may realize that the price he must pay is more than he is willing to give or that his goal is not very realistic. Any of these alternatives, arrived at by analyzing the facts objectively, is superior to the emotional reaction to subjective executive whim, misunderstandings, and rumors. Interviewing techniques should be used to create an open, two-way communication which permits an honest exchange of feelings, aspirations, and expectations. Young people want to level with a friendly authority who will guide their progress without moral lectures or illogical dogma.

CHAPTER SIX

Developing Potential Leaders

TRADITIONAL MANAGEMENT DEVELOPMENT TECHNIQUES have stood the test of time and often will prove effective with the younger generation, provided the process is speeded up to meet today's rapidly expanding management needs. The style of leadership exhibited by the superior also has an enormous impact on the motivation and learning or development of the young candidate. Finally, there are modern management development techniques designed and tested on the younger generation which are highly action-oriented and can produce more rapid personal development of potential leaders.

TRADITIONAL
MANAGEMENT DEVELOPMENT

The ancient craftsman-apprentice training system is the forerunner of most twentieth-century business training; however, the buddy system, as it is known today, rarely is used beyond the first job level. For example, novice salesmen are often trained by traveling with experienced salesmen, and this common training method often works out satisfactorily. But the salesman who is one day appointed to the sales manager's position rarely has the opportunity of serving as an apprentice manager under the immediate guidance and protection of his senior manager. There does not seem to be enough time to train a candidate in a one-teacher to one-pupil relationship in management. Either the newly appointed manager makes it on his own, or he is replaced by another candidate. This method of self-instruction by trial and error is very costly in terms of human resources and economy.

The more acceptable practice, common in business and industry for the past forty years, is basically the JIT (job instruction training) method. Traditionally, the learner is psychologically and emotionally prepared to want to learn, to appreciate the importance of the lesson, and to accept his trainer as an authority in his field. In the second step the material is presented by the instructor, and techniques are demonstrated with appropriate explanations. The trainer and the students go through the process together, with the instructor acting as a model of desired behavior. In the third step of the JIT process, the learner is required to demonstrate his knowledge and skill alone, as in a solo flight in pilot training. Finally, the learner is tested for mastery of the task and permitted to operate on his own with only periodic checks.

This method is superior to the craftsmen-apprentice training method because it does not freeze a man at a fixed level for a traditional time period. If the instructor feels the trainee is ready for dual flight, he proceeds. When the superior is reasonably confident the subordinate can solo, he gives him the opportunity to do so. In other words, the training is paced, in part at least, to the ability of the individual trainee, and one manager can bring along several trainees at the same time. This of course is very important when dealing with the newest generation in business.

MANAGEMENT BY EXCEPTION IN TRAINING

While management by exception is normally thought of as a strategy of operation, it is also a method of training and developing subordinates. The procedure is to break a complicated job down into a group of subtasks and teach a subordinate one subtask. When the subordinate masters that phase, he is given the authority to act as manager within the prescribed limits and held accountable for his actions and decisions. However, within the delegated sphere of operations he is completely on his own with only general supervision. As soon as he can operate comfortably within the first subtask, he is taught another subtask and the limits of his operation are broadened. As long as the problems and decision making are within the delegated limits, the subordinate is permitted to operate as he sees fit. When something occurs beyond the delegated sphere of authority, it is triggered to the attention of the superior.

Thus using management by exception as a training method, the superior delegates broader and broader authority and responsibility to the management candidate. He initially exercises close supervision or control as the candidate is learning but moves back to general supervision, such as routine reporting, as the younger man develops.

For example, a young man who has performed well on his initial assignments may be tentatively identified as future management potential. He may be given the authority and training to recruit additional young people. Once he performs his task satisfactorily, he may be given the authority and training to select and hire young people. His authority again may be broadened to enable him to recruit, select, hire, and train young people. Clearly, it can be broadened further to include the placement and supervision of some people, and sooner or later it must include the handling of older people.

Although each step has guidance from and control by higher management, the young man is encouraged to operate on his own within the delegated limits. He is closely supervised each time a new subtask is made his responsibility; however, as training permits, the superior spends less and less time watching and checking and more time in routine general supervision.

A superior manager knows each of his subordinates well

enough to recognize their individual goals in life. He knows when a young man is bored or when he is in danger of panic from being in over his head. The effective manager is able to identify which of the young man's goals are compatible with the manager's goals and with the company's goals. A good young man who wants a challenge as an opportunity to earn recognition is very trainable, and the effective manager knows his own promotion depends to a large extent on training his own replacement. The subordinate needs training, and this goal is compatible with the manager's goals and with the company's goals.

DELEGATION

There is a curious dichotomy in our social system today. On the one hand, people want to remain unique and differentiated individuals, while on the other hand they seek collectivism. People join together in nationalism. For example, note all the new countries admitted to the United Nations since World War II. Government agencies have grown to enormous size due to programs in health, education, and welfare. Labor unions have joined to form national and international bargaining units. With mergers and acquisitions, big business continues to create giant organizations. Big business, big labor, and big government simply cannot operate without delegating authority and responsibility. The amount of data generated by a large organization is beyond the comprehension of any one individual. If management does not delegate, it stifles its own growth.

Lack of delegation produces frustrated subordinates.

They may do a slow burn of anger, they may build resentment out of proportion to the cause, and good, capable people may quit. Equally damaging to an organization are those who withdraw emotionally and become complacent. In time, this situation leads to a house full of mediocre people. Competition is too keen to tolerate such attitudes and mediocrity for very long. Good young people are too hard to find, and it takes too long to develop them, to lose them by default.

An overall management development plan for an organization's growth will provide an orderly flow of people, trained and available to fill vacancies when the need arises. A good plan helps forecast and spotlight areas where training is necessary. It ensures everyone a chance to grow and develop. A well-executed plan will raise morale and increase loyalty because it brings people up from the ranks rather than use disruptive outside recruiting procedures.

The essence of management development planning is to provide the younger subordinates with the necessary experience they need to grow and mature. The understudy system may be appropriate for a few key jobs, but in general it is not applicable to an entire organization. A good plan will show when people will be needed, how many, and by whom. The pure system of understudies leads to duplication of the existing structure with little or no expansion.

Systematic job rotation will provide a general understanding of a large operation. It will often generate new ideas and encourage creativity, and it reduces the feeling of being trapped in one position. While applicable for a short term during training, it does not provide any incentives to perform in a superior manner; and because the individual knows he will be moving on, he has no roots or loyalty to a particular section or operation.

One very dangerous training approach is the "jet system," in which a promising young man is given rapid exposures and rapid promotions in an organization. Unfortunately he is not permitted time to make natural adjustments to people and to operations. His special treatment is seen by others as evidence that he is the crown prince who will soon lead. They will communicate to him only information that will look favorable, and they will hide, distort, or pass the buck on anything that might seem unfavorable. Thus the rising star is given a false education, and in the process he will sow many seeds of resentment and discontent among other employees.

Special broad assignments are often ideal to provide the essential experience the youngster needs to grow and develop. Putting a budget together or working on product development, for example, might require crossing department lines and viewing a situation broadly. The older manager should make it clear to the youngster that the results should not be simply adequate, which equates to unsatisfactory. The results expected should be clearly superior.

Bright young people can handle a number of special assignments with minimum supervision. Many are capable of designing market research studies, for example, and can conduct their own programs. Another area in which they can make an immediate contribution is in systems design, often involving the use of a computer. Whenever a fresh,

Falsely educating the rising star.

unbiased analysis is appropriate, these young people are
eager to serve.

MODERN
MANAGEMENT DEVELOPMENT

Having been raised in an affluent society with superior
knowledge and higher physical capabilities, the youngsters
are action-oriented and able to become totally involved or
totally uninvolved. When they are involved, or "turned
on," as young children are watching television cartoons,

they are literally oblivious to their environment. They do not see, hear, or think of anyone or anything else in the room. Conversely a poor speaker with a boring talk will drive their thoughts to a million other things, other places, and other people.

Because of the population explosion after World War II, our schools became overcrowded, and there was, and still is to a lesser extent, a critical shortage of qualified teachers. Educational costs are still skyrocketing, while the knowledge explosion doubles information every seven years. To solve this dilemma, two basic new educational tools have been developed: (1) video-tape recordings and (2) the computer in programmed learning and gaming or simulation. These tools have been researched, used experimentally, and finally used in mass education. Many of the young college graduates today are familiar with them, and in the next decade these tools will be very common.

VIDEO-TAPE RECORDING
IN TRAINING AND DEVELOPMENT

Because there is a shortage of good management, executives find they do not have the time to do all they should or would like to do. They would like to welcome new employees, give training and inspirational talks to workers, and provide regular communications about company goals, objectives, and policies. More and more executives in business are experimenting with inexpensive video-tape recording equipment for these purposes. The playback of video tape has a unique time dimension in that it gives the illusion of being live at this instant. The tape may have been made this morning, two weeks ago, or many months ago, but the viewer is not aware of the time lapse.

Video-tape replay also is unique in that the viewer feels the speaker is talking directly to him in a 1 to 1 ratio; he is not watching a motion picture, which he has been conditioned to feel is made for and played to the masses. This relatively intimate feeling permits total involvement if the speaker is effective and his target audience is known and understood. For example, a corporate president can make a tape welcoming new sales trainees in which he uses their language and refers to their initial assignments. The same tape could not be shown effectively to new engineers joining the same company. On the other hand, a plant tour could be video-taped with two narrations. One narration could be for the general public, pointing out the purity, efficiency, and production features. The second could be for new employees, noting the physical location of various technical operations and plant safety rules and regulations. Here one tape could serve a dual purpose, depending upon which sound track was played with the video.

Less commonly understood is the educational dimension of video-tape recording. Since many people do not like to read and most people have not been taught to listen effectively, a picture can often communicate better than either the spoken or the written word. The video tape can depict abstract concepts in cartoon form, with on-the-scene motion pictures, slides, or various forms of graphs, maps, and charts. Used with forethought, the video portion of the message can clarify or reinforce the spoken and written message. Models can be used to picture huge things, and close-ups can be used to magnify miniature things. The possibilities are limited only by the imagination of the creator and user of video-tape recording productions.

SELF-CONFRONTATION VIA
VIDEO-TAPE RECORDING

The major use of video-tape recordings in training in business and industry today is to provide a means to enable a man to see himself as others see him. This use has been termed "self-confrontation," because a man has the opportunity to see his own appearance, mannerisms, and behavior —literally to confront himself—as other people must do.

Sales training using role-playing episodes enables a trainee to try out various techniques with an instructor playing the role of a prospect. By reversing the roles, or making the sales trainee play the part of a prospect, a feeling of empathy or understanding of the buyer's position can be developed.

Interviewing techniques have been taught by using video-tape recording and role playing with instant replay for self-criticism and instructor analysis. Managers have been taught various leadership techniques and styles with video-tape recording, and trainers and general managers have been taught basic coaching techniques.

Human relations skills needed in management have been taught effectively with this new tool. The process may include questioning and probing techniques, effective listening skills, and effective communication techniques in giving out work assignments, conducting a group conference, and making a formal speech. One company uses video-tape recording role playing of case histories to teach techniques of delegation, motivating subordinates, and managing departments during periods of stressful change. Another company uses video-tape recording to teach techniques of control and discipline in a highly emotional situation. Others use it to train executives in conducting formal press conferences as well as off-the-cuff curbstone interviews. Again, applications are limited only by the imagination of the user of video-tape recording.

An American Management Association study by the author recently showed that while some older employees and executives disliked video-tape recording as a training tool, the younger, newer employees readily accepted it.[1] The young college graduates of today and for the next decade will seek the modern companies that use such action-oriented programs for self-development and training. Youngsters are impatient, and business can no longer afford the luxury of trial-and-error development when faced with a shortage of trained managers.

THE COMPUTER IN TRAINING AND DEVELOPMENT

It is a rare individual in the United States today who is not familiar with the scoring of a computer test. Early in

[1] Thomas F. Stroh, *The Uses of Video Tape in Training and Development,* American Management Association, New York, 1969.

grade school, children take intelligence tests that are scored by machine. As they advance in school, they are exposed to more and more machine-scored exams. At the college level many students are taught to communicate with computers either through computer-assisted instruction (CAI) or by playing a business game or simulating business conditions of uncertainty.

In computer-assisted instruction, the student identifies himself to the computer, which gives him a simple bit of knowledge and then asks a question. The student replies, and if his answer is correct, the computer gives him another bit of information, and so on. If the answer is wrong, the computer may rework the same information until the student gets the answer correct. This type of programming is called linear, and progress is in a straight line. More sophisticated programming analyzes a wrong answer of a series of wrong answers and instructs the student to go to an entirely different lesson before proceeding. This technique is called branch learning, and the computer adapts to each individual student. When a student returns for a later lesson, the computer's instant memory begins where it left off on the student's previous lesson.

The second major use of computers in education is in simulating a real business condition or in playing competitive games. In simulation, one puts data into a computer to duplicate as nearly as possible a real situation, such as population trends, economic forecasts, and the like, in an attempt to predict the results of various alternative actions. In games, the computer is programmed to receive the student's decisions regarding such things as production quantity, quality, advertising, market research, and so forth. Stu-

You will do as I say, cause I am the Boss!

dents represent competing companies, and each printout from the computer represents the resulting profit and loss statement and balance sheet for each company. The programs may permit many variables to interact, and they often permit the instructor to make sudden changes, such as removing a top producing salesman (he quit or was injured in an auto accident) to penalize or confuse a company.

Students who play such computer games become totally

involved and learn to make decisions under various conditions of uncertainty. They rise to the competitive challenge and, not incidentally, learn to analyze rapidly the financial data output from the computer. This type of learning is normally combined with lecturettes, case histories, and research assignments.

It should not be any wonder, then, that a bright young graduate joining business may be bored if he is told to sit passively and listen to lengthy orientation lectures or to study company manuals for weeks and months. Today's graduates are action-oriented and perform best when involved in the learning situation.

CONCLUSIONS

Because of the growing shortage of effective managers, traditional management training and development are neither economical nor efficient. They may very well work in many cases with the younger generation; however, in the next decade time will not permit such lengthy and individual training methods.

Using the concept of management by exception as a training and development vehicle will permit the total involvement of the young generation in meaningful and challenging work. It also enables the experienced senior manager to guide the development of a number of subordinates at various stages in their careers.

For optimum involvement and time efficiency, the management development climate should be combined with modern education tools. For areas concerning human relations and communications, the growing use of video-tape recording equipment is most applicable. For areas concerning analysis, synthesis, and decision making, there are many excellent games available. Both these training tools are readily acceptable by the younger generation and can be adapted to the individual or to large groups.

CHAPTER SEVEN

Communicating with the New Generation

WHEN EXPERIENCED MANAGERS ATTEMPT to interest and recruit the new generation into business, too often they fail to
communicate. When experienced executives attempt to listen to messages from youth, they often fail to understand
what they hear. Since business needs good young people
now in order to survive and grow, the burden of communication lies on the business executive. Once executives understand the psychology of communication, they should
have little difficulty in understanding and being understood by the younger generation.

103

PREDISPOSITION

Perhaps the largest difference between generations is not their knowledge and energies but their basic outlook on life. Young people are truly idealistic and impatient to change the world. They have vision and the daring will to innovate without regard to danger. They are at ease with change and look forward to an unknown future beyond imagination. With youthful enthusiasm and energy, they toss caution to the wind and are anxious to accomplish changes today. As a group, they are predisposed to action rather than the slow, deliberate, intelligent planning which older generations might call wisdom.

Predisposition is the collection of attitudes, opinions, beliefs, interests, and psychological needs of a person—the mental set of a person—before he is exposed to a message. It is the prior inclination, tendency, or susceptibility of a person to act or to become receptive before being stimulated. Predisposition is influenced by physical and economic needs as well as by social or group pressure, but the attitudes and opinions of an individual are based primarily upon his personality. The kind of person he is will most often determine how he will appraise a given situation and form his opinions.

There is some evidence that personality is formed partially through structural factors, physiological factors, and hereditary factors, but basically personality is developed through the learning process. If a young man persistently withdraws from many situations that demand adjustment, the reason is not that he belongs to a type but that his past learning has reinforced that kind of response.

Personality is learned primarily from experience with other human beings. Each person belongs to a number of social groups, and each group may affect his behavior in significant ways. Adults of the American culture speak English, have certain tastes in food and entertainment, and tend to put a high value on material success and personal ambition. Many European, African, and Asian adults have quite different norms and customs. In the same light, membership in a regional group, a church, a school, and a corner gang shape adjustment and influence the contours of personality through the contact such membership provides with other people and with their idea of how one ought to behave. In short, personality is, in large measure, a product of social learning.

The unique experience of each individual and its effect on his particular learning can be illustrated by the following story.[1] Assume three young college graduates were originally from the same neighborhood in New York City, were of the same nationality, attended the same church, and were members of the same corner gang. As young boys they all were unprepared for an approaching examination and became slightly ill. In one case, the mother liked to have her son home to baby and fuss over him. He learned that being sick can be a pleasant experience through which he

[1] This entire example is taken from Thomas F. Stroh, *Salesmanship: Personal Communications and Persuasion*, Irwin, Homewood, Ill., 1966, p. 93.

avoids facing an upsetting situation. Now he gets slight headaches to avoid facing business problems.

The second boy, also home sick, had an unpleasant experience because his mother nagged him and forced him to do extra homework as punishment. He learned being sick and staying home is worse than facing an unpleasant issue. As an adult, he now goes to work even when he shouldn't go, and he looks down on sick people as being weak and inferior.

The third boy complained to his mother about feeling sick, and she blamed his sickness on his being a bad boy who would not eat properly and therefore deserved to be sick. Sickness was a form of retribution for his wrongdoing. She gave him little or no sympathy. This boy learned to feel guilty whenever he was faced with an upsetting or unusual situation. Now, when the boss calls him in, he becomes uneasy and wonders what he has done wrong.

Personality is alive and continues to change with experience from birth to death. It is never so completely determined as to be unalterable. Children have the most to learn and are more docile, less critical learners; they therefore acquire many long-enduring behavior patterns. Later learning proceeds against a background of older adjustments that are strong because of effective and frequent reinforcements. Much of the later learning involves a modification of adjustment patterns rather than the acquisition of new ones. It is the entire cluster of learned attitudes of the personality which predisposes a young man to behave in a fixed or limited manner when faced with a situation involving conflict.

All personalities will vary quantitatively with respect to

various intensities of stress and also qualitatively with respect to particular areas of adjustment. A young man will react to certain ideas, people, words, and things, according to what his individual experience has taught him. These predetermined behavior patterns are both conscious and unconscious, sometimes rational and sometimes irrational, sometimes premeditated and sometimes impulsive, but they are predictable.

An executive should learn enough about each individual to know what meaning he is apt to apply to the executive's message and what emotional overtones he will infer. Feedback in a live interview is the key to open communication. The spoken objection or the unspoken expression on the face of the listener, the tone of his voice, his gestures, his general demeanor, or any combination of these constitutes feedback. The listener's reaction may be mild, intensive, passive, or aggressive, and the executive must be skillful in observing and evaluating it. He should adapt his message with a view to maintaining the young man's interest throughout. The executive can then become the friendly authority who helps the young man solve both organizational and personal problems that the youth himself recognizes. By sincere and honest means, the executive attempts to reeducate the youth in how to look at a problem, how to get around it and achieve his needs or goals, and how to tell the difference between what is and what might be.

DEFENSE OF PREDISPOSITION

Normally a person will go to extreme lengths to shield off attempts at changing his behavior and will resist in a

predictable behavior pattern. For example, young men con-
victed of minor traffic violations have been given a choice
of a haircut or so many days in jail, and, predictably, they
often choose the latter. Typically, a young man about to
graduate has already made certain decisions. He has decided to join an organization or not to begin a business career. He may have decided to join a particular company because he realizes certain satisfactions from dealing with its
executives or products. Any new executive or different organization is looked upon with suspicion and distrust by
the new graduate, and he will not readily examine his ha-
bitual way of maintaining his inner peace. Without realizing it, he may look for the phony, the misleading statements, the executive's lack of knowledge, the errors, the
excessive drinking, or anything else that he personally does
not like about people. He does this because the new executive represents a threat to his inner balance.

SELECTIVE EXPOSURE

One common defense against being changed or modified
is selective exposure, or the process of choosing messages
that promise to agree with and therefore to protect the predisposed attitudes of an individual. Young college men will
tend to expose themselves only to executives who can be expected to confirm their existing attitudes. Advance publicity or contact should indicate an area in which the young
people are already positively interested.

Young people will read certain magazines, such as *Playboy* and *Sports Illustrated,* and certain features, such as "Dear Abby," in local newspapers. They will listen to a certain radio station because it plays their kind of music. They will pay to see certain movies which promise to portray life as it really is. They do not watch much television other than programs with their favorite pop singers or modern comedy shows, both of which stress social inequalities and environmental abuses. Thus, for an organization to reach young people, it should gain selective exposure in appropriate media with a message that promises to discuss social inequalities or environmental abuses as they really exist.

If there is a single key to persuasion, it is confidence. The neophyte must learn to trust what the executive says before he will place any confidence in his offer or take any action the executive recommends. The effectiveness of various techniques of persuasion appears to be contingent on the *presumed* character of the message source. Studies have shown that sources which the audience holds in low esteem appear to constitute at least a temporary handicap to persuasion. What constitutes such esteem? Studies have shown that college-age audiences respond particularly well to specific sources because they consider them of high prestige, highly credible, expert, trustworthy, close to themselves, or just plain likable. Confidence in the source of a message seems to be a prerequisite to any persuasion attempt and should be the initial goal of the effective executive.

SELECTIVE PERCEPTION
AND RECALL

The next defense of predisposition involves selective understanding and selective memory of part of a message. An audience will hear and comprehend that with which it agrees and either not hear or not accept that with which it disagrees. The points of information one likes one can see at a glance, but points of disagreement are often unintelligible or not recognizable. The unwanted opinion or information is obscure or dark and of doubtful meaning or may seem ambiguous. This selective process is a defense of the mind which functions to filter our disagreeable information to protect one's self-image or one's preconceived beliefs and attitudes.

In addition to this defense filter, an audience also has a convenient memory in that it can easily recall the choice information contained in a message that is compatible with preconceived beliefs and attitudes. It will quickly forget or confuse those parts of a message which are contrary to existing beliefs. When tested for recall of a simple message of this type, an audience will not be sure of its content because the information didn't seem to make any sense to it or it felt the speaker could not be believed.

As an illustration, assume an executive states that his organization will pay a young man's travel expenses, hotel bill, and meals for a one-day visit to the headquarters office. At this time the young man repeats the offer and understands it perfectly well. One month later the young man

Which is most important?

makes the trip and stays for one week. When the organization says it will pay for only one night, the young man
reacts like a wounded bear: "But you told me you would
pay *all* my expenses! Why are you changing now?"

Is this young man a deliberate liar or a chiseler? Neither.
He is simply exhibiting the all too common human trait of
selective retention. In business parlance, this is referred to
as a convenient memory, and it is not confined to the
younger generation. Another illustration occurs all too frequently in a recruiter's promises. Most trained personnel

people are very careful in qualifying their statements about future salaries and promotions. They try to make it clear that nothing is guaranteed in this area and that only exceptional men rise rapidly. Young people are often overconfident and after a year on the job falsely assume the recruiter had promised them rapid promotions and pay raises regardless of their relative performance.

Executives seek to gain favorable attention, interest, and personal involvement on the candidate's part. Traditional managers go about it from their own self-centered point of view and ignore the young man's inner feelings. Words are the traditional manager's tools, and he attempts to use them to paint a word picture for youth to impress him and stimulate him with an emotional appeal.

Unfortunately, the result of the traditional manager's behavior is a complete lack of communication as the youth asks "stupid" questions or misunderstands the message completely. A number of social psychological studies have shown that the selective processes are the protective mechanisms that cause such misunderstandings, whether they are based on personal characteristics and prejudices or are based on economic and social beliefs and attitudes. A strong threat, such as discipline or fear on the new job, can also block subsequent communication.

REALISTIC COMMUNICATIONS OBJECTIVES

The modern manager, on the other hand, attempts to create effective communication with the young man. The manager has learned to *listen* rather than talk in order to learn the language the young man will understand. In a friendly manner, the modern manager attempts to get the new employee to discuss himself and so to dispel hostility. Through supportive feedback the manager creates a degree of kinship with the young man and therefore is most apt to get a reciprocal hearing from him when it is the manager's turn to talk.

For example, a young man on the job who is doing well may suddenly burst out in anger over some trivial thing. The modern manager will become a sympathetic listener and neutralize the young man's aggression. The manager will ask questions which encourage the subordinate to talk about his role in the organization and in his private life. Very often the younger man has made a minor mistake on the job and, because he is impatient, cannot forgive himself. The manager can then point out the nature of human beings and the way an intelligent man can learn by mistakes and get ahead faster than the man who is too cautious to try.

When the manager presents his message, he attempts to gain acceptance of one point at a time. He is continually alert to recognize the moment when the young man is mentally blocked. The manager decides instantly what to do about the problem while maintaining an open line to the other listener's mind—before he turns off. The selective processes generally serve to protect the young man's predisposition; however, they do not do so in all cases and on occasion may actually serve to encourage changing attitudes.

CONVERSION OF ATTITUDES

Young people behave as they do to satisfy conscious and unconscious needs of their bodies and minds, including contradictory desires and self-destructive drives. Inner goals may be rational or not, but however the inner attitudes are combined, people behave as they do because of these attitudes. In turn, the beliefs of an individual, his ideas, opinions, and attitudes, are based upon the social and economic realities of his situation as he understands them and his total learning experiences to that point in his life. For a person to change his behavior voluntarily, he must first change his attitudes or beliefs. Holding an attitudes serves the individual by enabling him to maintain his goal direction and not act at random against his own inner drives. This goal direction acts to maintain an inner balance or peace of mind. Wildly vacillating moods and seemingly incongruous behavior serve the total inner needs of the individual. Reviewed in this respect, all behavior is goal-directed and constant.

What psychological action takes place in the individual in whom an attitude changes? Something must have disturbed his inner balance which cannot be rectified internally without changing one or more attitudes. For example, additional knowledge about a girl friend may not be in keeping with a young man's previous attitude, and her new tarnished image will cause his attitude to change. Adjusting to new people and new situations may cause enough stress or anxiety to change attitudes in order to cope with the new situation.

Opinion conversion is the process which occurs when a minor or new attitude is elevated through reinforcement to dominate the matrix of attitudes, interests, and needs of a person. A seemingly new attitude is built up to the point at which it looms over all other attitudes and causes an individual to take some mental steps to regain his sense of inner balance. Normally any direct suggestion that an individual has false or wrong beliefs will alert his defense mechanisms to the point that he will discredit the accuser and disbelieve anything he might say in the future.

A persuasion attempt that begins with a minor point about which the listener is not aware of any particular feelings and then gains acceptance on this insignificant point has some chance of success. As minor points, seemingly of little or no consequence, are accepted, the effective defenses of resistance lie dormant.

As an illustration, many young people have little sense of monetary responsibility. They can damage another person's property with little or no remorse or guilt. They can often leave unpaid bills without a second thought. If one criticizes such behavior, a young man will not listen, or worse, he will attack the speaker. Conversely, if one asks a young man if he would like to be able to borrow $2,000 from a bank for a new car, the young man may very well become interested; certainly the topic is not a personal threat. The young man is apt to listen to credit requirements. The process of increasing an individual's tolerance for a new type of message seems to involve increasing his vague awareness and then his interest. He is then more apt to expose himself selectively to that type of communication and perceive and retain selectively more and more information which supports the new point of view. In due time, he may realize a good credit rating is a very desirable personal attribute, well worth seeking.

GROUP PRESSURES AND ATTITUDINAL CHANGES

The various groups to which an individual belongs tend to reinforce and protect his predisposition. This is particularly true of freshmen and sophomores in college. However, when the group no longer serves an individual's needs or seems to make sense, the same predisposition will encourage him to leave the group to find more satisfying norms elsewhere. This change seems to occur with more mature college people in their senior year as they consider leaving the campus.

Whatever the cause, as a young man's lot suddenly becomes unattractive in his own eyes, he will often look to new sources of information with a new set of attitudes totally out of keeping with his previous orientation. An analogous example might be the errant married executive who seems to break all previous ties and suddenly go off with his young blond secretary.

Opinion leaders, those whom the individual respects and listens to in a given field, will tend to present material biased by their own predisposition and will thereby influence the individual to change his own views to agree with the leader's opinions. If the young man respects a campus leader or his fraternity president, he may change his attitudes to conform to those of the leader. Often the flock waits for the leader's opinion before it will move. All successful conversion techniques depend primarily on lulling the defense mechanisms into inactivity and thereby gaining selective exposure, perception, and retention. Once having gained acceptance, new information is treated as if the person were predisposed to receive and enjoy it. Conflicting but subordinate attitudes can be reinforced to grow in strength to dominant positions, and the person effectively persuades himself.

NEW TO NEWEST GENERATION

When one visits a foreign country and cannot speak the language, he readily hires an interpreter to translate for him. Communicating with the newest generation can be accomplished through an interpreter; however, the problem is vastly more complicated than would appear on the surface. The generation gap which must be closed is no longer a father-son distance. The consensus of authorities is that *a generation is now about five years.*

Because of rapid technological changes, such as the third and fourth generation of computers, and the rapid development of knowledge, two men graduating from the same school five years apart are figuratively a generation apart. The speed with which newspapers, radio, and television report events in distant countries makes the newest generation the most knowledgeable because the older man out of school four or five years is now preoccupied with earning a living. Thus if an executive wishes to hire an interpreter to talk to the newest generation, he should make sure the interpreter speaks the current language.

CONCLUSIONS

The psychology of communication and persuasion is based on the principle that all behavior is goal-directed. People are predisposed to act in a predictable manner according to what they have learned up to that point in their lives. They have a mental set.

The individual strives to maintain an inner balance and defends himself against any change which might upset his mental status quo. Common defenses include selective exposure, or listening only to someone who agrees or promises to agree with the predisposition. Selective perception and retention are the mental defenses which filter out those parts of a message which do not agree with the predisposed attitudes. Selective recall is the defense which enables a person to recall easily the agreeable and confuse or forget quickly the disagreeable.

By listening to a young man, an executive can learn both the language and the inner motivation of the individual. Gaining the other man's confidence and respect should be the primary objective of the manager. Then when he presents his message, the manager can use language which the subordinate will understand. The manager can develop a minor point and gain acceptance, gradually reinforcing this position without alerting the psychological defenses.

As the young man's lot becomes unattractive in his own eyes, he will often look to new *credible* sources of information and guidance. Thus conflicting but subordinate attitudes can be reinforced to grow in strength to dominant positions, and the young man effectively persuades himself.

Finally, in using a young employee to recruit on campus, executives should be aware of the fact that a generation, in this context, is about five years. Beyond this limit, the interpreter may not speak the current language.

CHAPTER EIGHT

Living with the New Generations in the Future

IN 1970, THERE WERE approximately 22 million students in high schools and colleges, and by 1975 the number is expected to exceed 25 million. These students will be part of tomorrow's management. Each generation in our modern society benefits from the research and development as well as the economic savings of prior generations. Medical science will continue to make each succeeding generation superior to its predecessor. The physical sciences will continue to produce superior tools for future generations. The social sciences will provide ever-expanding knowledge in geometric progression for man's future in his own environment and in space. Man should be proud of this age of light and enlightenment.

MANAGERIAL
QUALIFICATIONS IN 1980

Hindsight is often twenty-twenty vision. It is relatively easy to look back, after the facts are known, and point out mistakes and show how a different action would have been better. Looking forward or forecasting with various degrees of uncertainty can be quite hazardous. Given such an obvious generalization, there are existing facts in 1970 which point to the occurrence of certain events in the next decade. For example, all the people who will be in management in 1980 have already been born, and their personalities are now well developed. Most of them by 1975 will have completed their formal education. Certain technologies which are now in existence will be mass-implemented in the next

"*I started as a simple mechanic, and now . . .*"

five to ten years. Public conscience for social justice, environmental safety and control, and rapid international communication and transportation are now in various stages of development and mass acceptance. Decisions that will affect tomorrow's managerial success must be made today on the basis of partial information.

For example, successful managers of the future will have a broad knowledge and appreciation of social values. They will be well aware of their organization's contribution to or impact on the local, regional, and international community. They will develop ways and means to measure an organization's social capital in much more meaningful terms than today's catchall term "goodwill."

In addition to having a broad knowledge of the social sciences, tomorrow's successful managers will be relatively sophisticated in the field of the behavioral sciences including psychology, education, sociology, and other combined disciplines. The knowledgeable managers of the future will not make the mistakes we made in the 1960s in dealing with individuals, groups, and masses of people.

A third major difference in future managers will be their competence in the quantitative sciences and in relating their technical competence to the real world. In management seminars today, we refer to this area as "SWAG," or the science of wild asinine guesses. Technology and computer simulations will reduce guesswork in the future, and the quantitative sciences will take their place.

A fourth managerial qualification of the 1970s will be a worldwide perspective rather than today's regionalism and nationalism. Organizations such as Europe's Common Market will no longer serve the international concern operating around the world. As countries leap from an agrarian economy directly to a technological economy, they will need and demand different products, services, and financing. Government support for the importer and exporter will be essential, and the more effective managers will be both knowledgeable and highly aware of the intricacies of operating on a worldwide basis.

A fifth qualification for tomorrow's managers will be understanding and willingness to accept the need for continuous learning. In a period of rapid technological advancement, existing knowledge becomes obsolete in a matter of a very few years. New management tools must be mastered as they become available. As the development of new knowledge accelerates, one can no longer afford the time-consuming trial-and-error method of learning. Obsolescence will quickly overtake the managers who hesitate to learn continuously.

Finally, the managers of tomorrow will have a strong sense of morality and humanity. In the 1960s, managers were concerned primarily with scientific management or efficiency and with improving the standard of living or material possessions of people. By 1980, successful managers will be concerned with protecting humanity or man's decency and improving the quality of life.

Admittedly, these broad predictions of successful managers in 1980 are in the category of SWAG, but they seem realistic to the author. If they are valid to a small degree, they certainly point up the true contribution which youth can make to any organization of the future.

DEVELOPMENT OF
YOUNG PEOPLE

Since the young really are healthier, more energetic, more knowledgeable, more international in viewpoint, and often more moral then their elders, management should not only permit but encourage the young to take over and assume responsibility sooner. They are ready and able to make sound business decisions at least as well as, if not better than, existing management in most concerns. They are certainly more advanced in their sense of social responsibility and in their sincere concern regarding the pollution and exploitation of man's environment. Are they willing? A few of the rising young men in business are not only willing but impatient to assume more and more responsibility. They are being drawn into the vacuum of the ever-increasing shortage of management. Handled appropriately, they will contribute immensely to the growth of business for the benefit of mankind. They must be given the opportunity to make mistakes, just as the student jet pilot must be given the opportunity to solo in a $1 million aircraft. One would not expect the student pilot to fly as expertly as the veteran pilot, but if he is trained properly, he will fly safely. One should not expect the junior executive in charge of a $1 million operation to administer it as well as the veteran executive, but if he is trained properly, he will run it satisfactorily.

Mistakes may be costly; however, they provide golden opportunities to educate junior executives in a climate that

Reach out and take charge!

encourages growth. If the young are not given this opportunity to err, they should not be expected to learn. If they are
reprimanded or disciplined for mistakes, they may learn
taking a risk is not worth the possible rewards. They may
lose the self-confidence which is essential in the decision-
making process. If they are brought along in appropriate
steps, they can *average* better decisions in a shorter time period than their elders. Only the extreme egotist in business
today pretends he is infallible. In life, every man makes
mistakes and must live with the consequences. Given
proper guidance, the younger generations will not make all

the same mistakes of their predecessors, but they will make mistakes. Accepting this reality, senior executives can create a business atmosphere which encourages a young man to reach out, take charge, and assume responsibility.

A much larger group of college seniors who are ready and able to assist business are not particularly willing to start. As noted earlier, this attitude is due in part to their lack of understanding of the real opportunities to help mankind and the real challenges to their mental abilities. It is also due in part to the feedback from recent graduates who entered business and were placed in menial jobs or were placed under a harried middle manager who feared their rapid success. Perhaps the greatest deterrent to joining business is the well-publicized articles on the demands and pressures of executive life.[1] While labor unions have won the four-day workweek, executives average more than fifty hours per week in the office and an additional ten hours of work at home. Executive travel has been increased by the age of the jets, and wives and children resent the time Dad spends on the road. In contrast to popular belief, the United States ranks low in longevity: twenty-fourth among countries that keep statistics. Male life expectancy, 66.7 years, has not risen significantly in the United States since the 1940s. Some authorities state this is due in part to the pressure to perform well in business, and many young graduates are questioning the price of business success.[2] Brought

[1] Janet Smith, "Can Companies Reduce Heart Attacks?" *Dun's Review*, April, 1970, p. 51.
[2] Susan Margetts, "Executives: Taut, Tense, Cracking Up," *Dun's Review*, March, 1969, p. 54.

up in an affluent society, our intelligent young people do ask such fundamental questions.

A recent international study of managers in fourteen countries clearly points up the age problem in our business society.[3] Of all 3,641 managers who responded, those under thirty years of age in each country sampled were as follows:

	% of total population
Norway	0
Sweden	1
France	1
United States	2
Japan	2
Belgium	4
Denmark	6
England	7
Germany	8
Argentina	12
Spain	16
Italy	18
Chile	23
India	32

It would seem that the solution of this problem brings one full cycle to the original question: "Who needs the young people in business?" Clearly, with a shortage of good management people and the demands of growth, executives need the help of youth if they expect to survive. Given complete information, young people will recognize both the opportunities and the challenges of the real business world, and they will come to the aid of their elders.

Living with the new generations in the future will require constant reevaluation of training programs and time

[3] Mason Haire, Edwin E. Ghiselli, and Lyman W. Porter, *Managerial Thinking: An International Study*, Wiley, New York, 1966.

periods for various development assignments. The young of today are not experienced; hence they really do need guidance and opportunities for self-development. Behind the facade of brashness, young people subconsciously seek guidance. They are very willing to listen to a friendly authority who will state the facts as they exist. They do *not* want a big brother to protect them as in traditional paternalistic management. And it would be a foolish manager who would accept youth's brash demands and abdicate power to the neophyte. What the young of today are honestly seeking is guidance to develop their potential and an opportunity to contribute as rapidly as they prove themselves able.

PLANNING

A major function of management is planning. One sign of poor management is a superior who does the same work as his subordinates instead of spending time on long- and short-range plans. Planning includes not only the obvious formulation of goals but a philosophy of ethics appropriate to achieve goals as well as information systems which permit the group to stay on target.

Young people today can contribute to planning in at least two of the three areas noted. They are very conscious of water and air pollution, urban problems, and man's responsibility to his fellow man. To include their views in formulating a philosophy of ethics to achieve goals would be very sound planning. Common objectives, specific tasks, time deadlines, and measurement systems can be planned by our young people.

As noted earlier, these bright young people are system-oriented, and many have been taught computer techniques to handle masses of data intelligently. With some guidance by experienced executives, the young people can assist in areas that the older managers may hesitate to explore. The systems approach is comfortable for young people, and many can help in this part of the planning function.

ORGANIZING

Industry trends toward centralizing and decentralizing authority tend to swing like a clock pendulum. Often, a change is made simply to excite the people in a tradition-bound company. In either case, delegation is essential if a company is to grow. People must be developed by having them assume more and more responsibility and authority.

Properly trained, young people can and will accept responsibility. They readily respond to job enlargement as they learn. They do rise to meet their superiors' higher levels of expectation. They will accept staff assignments, follow procedures, and communicate as instructed once they understand how their subtask relates in importance to the total objective.

One organizational trend which will continue in the 1970s is the task force management concept. While older executives may decry management by committee, young people respond very well to multiple assignments and reporting to more than one authority. They want to be where the action is, and they really have boundless energy to contribute. Their college experiences have predisposed them to operate in this manner.

LEADERSHIP

While leading social scientists encourage permissive styles of management, they often generalize to the point of pressing this extreme to the exclusion of all other styles of leadership. What is lost in the debate is the appropriateness of a given style of leadership to the experience level and competence of the audience. Young people can and do respond favorably to the friendly authority. Older experienced people do realize there are many possible courses of action in a complex situation, and they are willing to accept the decisions of top management.

Different styles of leadership for different situations and for different followers are not only acceptable to subordinates but highly desirable from the standpoint of effectiveness. Given good two-way communications between the manager and subordinates, the employees will be motivated to achieve the level expected of them. Most people who have not given up hope of self-improvement are ready and willing to learn more, to accept authority and responsibility, to grow and develop. Clearly, this general statement is most applicable to our young college graduates, and the style of leadership should encourage a climate of growth.

The leader's responsibility is to synchronize the team effort and relate it to accepted company goals. He leads by example, by superior knowledge, and by rewarding outstanding performance.

CONTROL

The fourth function of management is control, both budgetary and nonbudgetary. Accounting and financial reporting are taught to our youngsters in college, and they readily understand and accept such controls. There are no surprises in this area, and often the young man can assist in making a business system more sophisticated and more meaningful.

The nonbudgetary controls to identify points of friction and work-flow bottlenecks include sophisticated manpower planning concepts and attempts to evaluate various training and development experiences. One of the biggest assets of a company may be the employee's loyalty and technological knowledge; yet this rarely shows in the traditional balance sheet or operating statement. Such new areas of measurement and control would be highly challenging to our young people, and they should be able to contribute here.

REWARDS TO
EXISTING MANAGEMENT

By recruiting and developing today's youth in business, existing middle management and top executives will gain an increase in production or output. By giving youth's boundless energies direction, business can harness its power and construct better establishments. Young people will work hard to achieve their goals; however, their methods may be very different from the older ways of doing things. If they can achieve more, perhaps sooner, then the change may very well be for the better.

In the process of doing things their way, not necessarily the boss's way, young people will want to know the reason why certain methods are used and the purpose of various information collected and data reported. Young people today will not accept the standard: "There is no reason for it; we have always done it that way." They are rightly inquisitive and may drive executives to distraction, but they will increase marketing efficiency and profits. Information which is not needed will be discarded and that which is essential may be obtained more quickly in more easily understood form and more accurately. Cost savings will be achieved in areas where other managers have been blinded by traditional training.

In the process of increasing production and efficiency, generating profit, reducing costs, and reducing paper work, the young businessman will make existing management look *better* than it really is or can ever hope to be without youth. Because young people do need guidance and planned sequences of varied experiences, middle management people who successfully aid in their training and development will gain the recognition of top executives and the promotion which they also seek. They will also build a loyal staff of young people who will lighten the load now and in years to come.

Finally, there is a tremendous personal satisfaction in knowing that you have been instrumental in the constructive development of a young person who goes on to success. Academicians, since the ancient Greeks, have known the pride of seeing their students achieve greatness, realizing that a piece of the teacher will live on in the youth. Today's youth will give the manager a tremendous sense of pride and the day-by-day satisfaction on the job which comes from the successful training and development of others.

CHAPTER NINE

Mixing Young
and Old Managers

MANY EXPERIENCED AND COMPETENT SENIOR MANAGERS fear or distrust the young newcomer to their organization. Too often, the more intelligent and ambitious the young man might be, the greater the threat he becomes for some older managers. Just as old equipment, machinery, and systems become obsolete, managers also grow obsolete. Some managers remain on a given level of performance while their jobs grow beyond their competence. Other managers may actually improve their performance but still are unable to keep pace with competition. All managers need to update themselves continually or risk obsolescence.

Top management in a company must establish a climate of healthy growth and development for all its employees, at all age levels. The principles of modern management are

135

not limited to dealing with the young generation alone. They are equally appropriate for older managers: the two groups can and should be mixed together.

Typical treatment of less effective managers in business and industry is to reduce their authority by transferring part of their job to others. Also common, but less desirable, is the transfer or relocation of ineffective managers, including the promotion of incompetents.[1] In many companies, termination is the most common method of solving executive obsolescence. Thus, an older manager's fear of bright and ambitious trainees is not simply a figment of his imagination but a true reflection of top management's traditional policy![2] Traditional management practices have contributed to the current shortage of middle management. Traditional practices have also contributed to the short life-span of the United States male. Business and industry are rapidly reaching the point of no return. Either modern management principles are to be applied in the 1970s, or American business itself will stagnate and stifle its own life. When individuals stop growing, they begin dying, and in our technological society obsolescence will come much more quickly. If middle management is asleep or too frightened to act, this condition is a direct reflection of top management.

[1] Laurence J. Peter and Raymond Hull, *The Peter Principle,* Morrow, New York, 1969.

[2] Frederick C. Haas, *Executive Obsolescence,* American Management Association, New York, 1968.

USING OLDER
MANAGER'S CAPABILITIES

Given a relatively competent and loyal middle manager who shows behavioral signs of becoming obsolete in the future, what can top management do with him? Take the manager who no longer wants to assume any risk or who is content with things as they are instead of keeping up with technological knowledge or who, perhaps, has less physical stamina; this manager needs help. He has been tried and proved capable; hence it would be imprudent to relieve him of authority and inhumane to terminate his employment. In addition, the shortage of managers is already acute.

As noted earlier, a company with clearly written goals and objectives can write job descriptions and manpower specifications for every management position in the organization. If an experienced manager wants a promotion, he can be shown exactly what knowledge and skills are required before he is eligible for that promotion. If he is not performing adequately on his current job, this can be pointed out very objectively and fairly. If his job is to grow in the next few years, he can see what new technical knowledge he will have to acquire to maintain a satisfactory level of performance.

To paraphrase Fred Herzberg's KITA theory, one need not be kicked to move. A dog biscuit (reward) will move a subordinate just as well as a kick (punishment). But in nei-

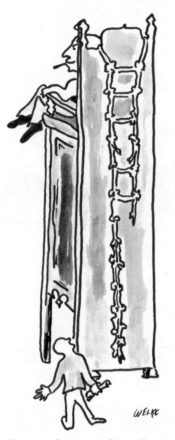

How can I grow to the top?

ther case is the subordinate motivated—only the one who administers the kick.[3] The middle manager needs something within himself to grow, to become better, to contrib-

[3] Fred Herzberg, *Work and the Nature of Man,* World, Cleveland, 1966. See also Fred Herzberg, "The New Kid in the Company," *Innovation Magazine,* December, 1969.

ute to the welfare of others. He needs a realistic chance to achieve and earn recognition for accomplishment. Traditional management practices of reward and punishment do not work with the new generation and certainly have failed too often with older managers in the past.

Most middle managers can and will improve themselves once they are convinced lip service alone is not enough. Once the need for positive, effective action is accepted, ongoing management development programs can provide middle management with capabilities that are lacking.

EQUAL TREATMENT
FOR THE YOUNG

The motivation techniques of reward and punishment are becoming obsolete. Material rewards, to be sure, are still important, but only if they are not provided. When they are provided, they become relegated to a secondary status in Maslow's hierarchy of needs in motivation.

For example, a thirty-one-year-old division manager should be paid on the basis of his responsibility and performance exactly the same as a fifty-one-year-old division manager. If he is not compensated for his performance, clearly he will be susceptible to offers from another organization.

Above and beyond cash, an organization should offer opportunity—the chance to assume responsibility at a very early age. It should offer continuing education for the total development of all employees as people. Instead of avoiding civic and political involvement, an organization should encourage its employees to seek political office if they wish. Those who are successful should not be given special privileges but still be expected to carry a full work load on the job.

A young man with a staff job, as an assistant to one of a company's ranking vice-presidents, for example, is exposed to a number of different corporate problems in a short space of time. He can serve as a legman between headquarters and field operations. His energy, good health, and ambition can serve the senior executive under the latter's control and guidance.

An organization may also rotate a young executive through a certain sequence of jobs in order to prepare him to assume higher responsibility and to supervise men who will be his seniors. For example, after broad corporate exposure, a young man may be assigned the job of evaluating a potential acquisition. If top management approves his recommendation to acquire a company, the young man can be put in charge of one function for the subsidiary. To earn the respect of older, more experienced men in the subsidiary, the young man would have had corporate headquarters experience, possibly some international exposure, and the current research knowledge of the new industry. He would also have the confidence of headquarters top management.

HOW DO OLDER
PEOPLE REACT?

As one would expect, some older men will refuse to give the younger men a chance to sell themselves. Some will try to buck the promotion of young men. When they do, top management should ask them to give the policy a trial. Most older men will be willing, but a few will quit.

The older men should be made aware that they can grow too. Often they will, once they know it is expected. They will be helped and trained, and they will be exposed to a number of bright young men asking questions. There are some anxieties and qualms in older people's minds when a young man comes in over them. It is up to the youth to develop a relationship that will make the older person willing to give him a chance to prove himself. Then the young man must demonstrate by actions and decisions that he really does have the talent which the older subordinates need for their own success.

Obviously, some older men will quit, and some younger ones will not make good and may have to be fired. Generally it is the degree of emotional maturity—the ability to predict what others will think, or sensitivity to others' reactions—which will determine the degree of success of the young person.

An organization needs seasoned executives. There is an educational process which experience provides that cannot be accelerated in the classroom. To overcome obstacles, an impatient young man is apt to compromise when he should stand and argue with the majority. An older executive, who may not have the necessary energy and ambition to fight the battle, can advise and encourage the younger man to stand and fight where it will do the organization the most good.

LEVEL OF EXPECTATION

Just as young people will perform poorly if they are expected to do so and perform in a superior manner if that is what is expected of them, so too will experienced middle managers. A mature man will learn how to use new management tools, such as the computer, if he knows his boss has confidence in him, is willing to train him, and fully *expects* him to learn. If the mature middle manager is not given the training and support he needs, he is probably correct in assuming his superiors do not really expect him to learn. People, young and old, will move of their own accord to meet the level of expectation of their superiors. And they will do so without reward or punishment.

Unfortunately, the subordinate's assumption of the level of performance expected by the superior may not agree with the true level of expectation. For this reason alone, defining goals, jobs, and manpower specifications and other management methods are essential to understanding. Establishing a climate for growth which permits mistakes in the learning process is also a key ingredient in this process. Given an understanding of the need to learn and a climate in which to become better, a mature manager will be self-motivated to rise to meet the true expectations of top management. Conversely, if top management assumes a man in his forties or fifties cannot learn new technological methods, middle management will not learn, at least with that particular company.

Douglas McGregor taught a similar business philosophy through his theory of extremes.[4] If the manager feels subordinates must be constantly pushed or pulled to get them to move, they will not react unless there is a reward or punishment. In either event, the subordinate is not motivated—only the boss. At the other extreme, if the manager feels subordinates will plan, create, and act on their own, they will do so with little help from the boss. The manager is around only to assist the worker, not to supervise or criticize. Perhaps this theory is exaggerated to make the point (as we often do in education), but it is another illustration of the phenomenon that people do move to meet the level of performance expected by their superiors. This kind of behavior has been studied and documented in business, industry, government, and education for many years. Almost all job levels and almost the complete span of life and business experience tend to confirm this principle of the level of expectation.

MANAGEMENT BY EXCEPTION

A mature middle manager who shows signs of early obsolescence normally is reflecting learning which has been reinforced most of his life. Just as a young person must be taught subtasks first and larger tasks gradually in time, so should the mature executive be brought along in the same manner. If a complete reversal in behavior is expected over-

---

[4] Douglas McGregor, *The Human Side of Enterprise*, McGraw-Hill, New York, 1960.

night, such an expectation will be overwhelming to both the young neophyte and the mature executive.

If a job description must be changed to meet new conditions and the manpower specifications upgraded, then a realistic timetable should be established for the incumbent manager to acquire the new knowledge and skills. In certain areas he should be permitted to operate without supervision as he has in the past, but in other areas, where change is expected, he should have instruction and close supervision for each phase of the learning process. As he achieves the desired level of performance on the subtask, the superior then permits the manager to operate on his own with only general supervision. As each phase is completed, the middle manager's job is broadened more and more with fewer and fewer exceptions being brought to the immediate attention of his superiors. In this way, management by exception can be an excellent vehicle to retrain and broaden a mature middle manager.

Written job descriptions and manpower specifications can be objective and much more easily accepted emotionally than can a seemingly subjective opinion of a superior. A middle manager in his forties or fifties has the emotional strain of his own body chemical changes, his maturing family, and financial demands which may seem overpowering to him. Rumors of job changes may be viewed as a threat. Therefore, the more objective and clearly communicated the expected new levels of job performance are, the more apt the manager is to accept change and improve himself.

PARTICIPATION IN
DECISION MAKING

Of course, some mature executives will not be willing or able to modify their behavior for a number of legitimate and human reasons. If they are capable in limited areas of value to the organization, then a new written job description can be related to the organization's objectives with limited authority and responsibility spelled out in detail. A bright young college graduate can be assigned to assist the mature executive in the areas the older man cannot learn, such as computer simulations. For all the advances in scientific management, mature experience is still an essential ingredient in the art of management. The young and the old can and should work together in management.

Rather than having the older manager fear and resist changes, permit him to guide new systems and applications of new tools and enter new business situations. This can be done rather easily once his old job responsibilities have been limited. His released time can be utilized to the organization's advantage by assigning the executive to a number of task force groups. Here the mature executive is expected to influence, but not direct, his younger associates, and top management should make this distinction clear to all members of the task force.

Such task force assignments indicate top management's respect for the senior manager, and they can be rewarding emotional experiences for the older manager. He will feel needed and can make many legitimate contributions to his company. In the long run, this is much more economical to the company than living with incompetence or promoting a man out of a job. Of course, it is also humane, and this pays off in better employee morale and loyalty throughout an organization.

CONCLUSIONS

Population statistics are now available for all people who will be in management for the next twenty years. One need not wonder about shortages of effective managers. We have a shortage in 1970, and we will have a more acute shortage in 1975, which will not ease before 1980.

American organizations must deal more effectively with their senior managers if they are to grow. Early retirement and promoting incompetent people are both expensive and wasteful of the human resources so badly needed. Traditional management practices of reward and punishment do not motivate people in the positive sense, and these practices in the past have taught too many managers not to risk change.

This decade began with a sharp change in the public conscience regarding business and the environment in which we live. Water and air pollution and social injustices are just a beginning of the many problems which will require changes in business in this decade. The knowledge explosion together with radically improved worldwide communications into the home will accelerate executive obsolescence. Adapting to change is essential for organizations which desire to survive and grow. Clearly, the old traditional management practices have passed the point of being useful.

Modern management principles which truly motivate the inner man and utilize more of his innate capabilities will produce a better, more responsive business society. They will permit a man to realize satisfaction in doing his job and, it is hoped, will enable him to live a longer, healthier life.

In the same context, the new generation coming into business and industry will respond positively to these modern management principles. Our young people are bigger, healthier, and more knowledgeable than older generations. Perhaps most important, they bring new social consciousness to business and a worldwide perspective which will be sorely needed in the 1970s. Our young people can help solve many of our business problems, and they should be most welcome.

Appendix

According to a recent survey by the writer, the following is
a partial list of computer games and simulations played in
business and at universities in the United States and Can-
ada:

LOCATION AND GAMES	APPLICATION	LEVEL
Dartmouth College:		
Uniproduct	Production management	Master
Top Brass	Business policy	Master
MEDIA	Marketing management	Master
Macro/Micro	Economics	Master
GLOOM	Economics	Master

LOCATION AND GAMES	APPLICATION	LEVEL
Fresno State College:		
Boston College Decision Making Exercise	Marketing	Master
Georgia Institute of Technology:		
IBM Game for 7094 Computer	General management	Master
Northwestern University:		
UCLA	Marketing	Bachelor
Northwestern	Marketing	Master
Purdue	Accounting, marketing	Bachelor
Gremex	Production	Master candidate
Queen's University:		
Queen's Executive Game	General management	Bachelor and Master
Project "Decide"	Production planning	Master
State University of New York at Buffalo:		
UCLA Game Model #3	General management	Master
Carnegie Institute of Technology	Marketing, management	Bachelor and Master
Locally programmed management simulation	General management	Bachelor and Master
University of Chicago:		
INTOP	General and international business	Master of business administration
University of North Carolina:		
The Executive Game	All areas	Bachelor
The Carnegie Tech Management Game	All areas	Master

LOCATION AND GAMES	APPLICATION	LEVEL
University of Toronto:		
Own games	Production	Bachelor
	Finance	Master
Bank of Commonwealth:		
Proof and Transit Simulation Model	Banking	Bachelor or above
Borg-Warner:		
IBM Management Decision	Marketing	Bachelor or master
Chesapeake and Ohio Railway Company:		
Train Performance Calculator	Over-the-road railroad operation	All levels
Single Track Capacity Analyzer	Over-the-road railroad operation	Bachelor
Terminal Model II	Railroad terminal operation	
Chrysler Institute:		
Dealership Management Simulation	Participants plan and evaluate as they would do in all areas of their dealerships	Level not listed
Crown Zellerbach Corporation:		
IBM Decision Makers	Overall business orientation	Bachelor
Max	Sales territory planning	Bachelor
Quaker Oats	Supermarket management, retail food store management	Bachelor

LOCATION AND GAMES	APPLICATION	LEVEL
Data Service Bureau:		
GPSS	Traffic patterns diamond interchange	Professional engineer
SCERT	Computer system evaluation	Two-year analyst, one-year computer
Diamond Power:		
System 360 Management Decision	Sales, manufacturing, engineering, accounting	Level not listed
Eli Lilly and Company:		
IBM Business Game, Model 30 DOS	Corporate finance	All levels
F. S. Services:		
Purdue Farm Supply Business Management Game	Used as production inputs for farming	High school and bachelor
General American Life:		
GRASP	Profit planning, competitive strategies, sales forecast, budgeting	Bachelor
General Electric:		
Own games	Manufacturing/ employee relations, general employee relations, and union negotiations, marketing strategy	For operating GE managerial personnel

LOCATION AND GAMES	APPLICATION	LEVEL
IBM Corporation:		
FAME	Production, marketing, finance	Executive development
MANAGE	Production, marketing, finance	Customer executive
Insurance Company of North America:		
INA Management Game	Insurance, service office operations	Bachelor
Koppers Company, Inc.:		
Marksim	Marketing and business	Marketing personnel
Lenkurt Electric Company, Inc.:		
Production and Inventory Simulation	Production and Inventory planning	Bachelor
Price Break Analysis	Purchasing	Bachelor
Manufacturers Hanover Trust:		
IBM Bank Management Simulation	Bank management	Bachelor
Metropolitan Life:		
SOLID	Life insurance	All levels
Minnesota Mutual Life Insurance Company:		
Minnesota Mutual Life Insurance Management Game	Life insurance	Bachelor
Price Waterhouse & Company:		
Budget Problem- Interactive	Executive and financial management	Management level

LOCATION AND GAMES	APPLICATION	LEVEL
Quaker Oats:		
Supermarket Management Decision Making Game	Retail food store operations	Store management personnel
Quaker Sales Simulator	Quaker sales management personnel	Sales management
United States Gypsum Company:		
Linear Programming Transportation Model	Distribution problems	Level not listed

Index

Index